COLD SWEAT

COLD SWEAT

My Father James Brown and Me

Yamma Brown

with Robin Gaby Fisher

CHICAGO
REVIEW
PRESS

An A Cappella Book

Published by Chicago Review Press, Incorporated
814 North Franklin Street
Chicago, Illinois 60610
ISBN 978-1-883052-85-0

Library of Congress Cataloging-in-Publication Data
Brown, Yamma, author.
  Cold sweat : my father James Brown and me / Yamma Brown, Robin Gaby Fisher.
    pages cm
  Includes index.
  Summary: "Yamma Brown was one of James Brown's daughters. The struggles she
went through, both as a child and as an adult, provide a profound examination of
the nature of celebrity, violence, and survival"—Provided by publisher.
  ISBN 978-1-883052-85-0 (hardback)
  1. Brown, James, 1933–2006. 2. Brown, Yamma. 3. Soul musicians—United
States—Biography. I. Fisher, Robin Gaby, author. II. Title.

ML420.B818B76 2014
782.421644092—dc23
[B]

                                    2014006952

Interior design: PerfecType, Nashville, TN
Photo credits: All photos courtesy of Yamma Brown

Printed in the United States of America
5 4 3 2 1

CONTENTS

1

Your Father's Dead

"The bitterest tears shed over graves are for words left unsaid and deeds left undone."

—Harriet Beecher Stowe, Little Foxes

I'D FINALLY FINISHED wrapping all the kids' Christmas presents and had just dropped off to sleep when the sound of the phone ringing shattered the silence of my bedroom. A phone call in the middle of the night is never good news. I froze for a second before picking up. "Hello? This is Yamma," I said, hearing the breathlessness in my voice. I recognized Mr. Bobbit's low Southern drawl right away. "Yaaammaa dear, your father is dead," he said plaintively. I gasped and threw the phone down, as if the receiver had dealt the shock that bolted through my body. "My father is dead!" I cried. "Oh no! God, please!" My husband, Darren, sat up in bed next to me. He tried to pull me close to comfort me, but I pushed him away. I was inconsolable. Tears gushed down my cheeks. My sobs turned to long, sorrowful howls. The anguish I felt shook my entire being. "I'm sorry," Mr. Bobbit said.

Charles Bobbit was my father's longtime personal manager. He had been at his bedside at Emory Crawford Long Hospital in Atlanta that night in 2006 when Dad's heart just gave out, he said. The doctors had tried valiantly to revive him but with no success. Dad was gone. How could it be true? I had just spoken with him by phone the day before. "Don't worry, Yamma," he'd said. "I'm getting better. I'll be out of here in a day or two." Dad had assured me then that the hospital stay would be brief, because he was going on tour right after Christmas. His doctors had already approved the trip. Yes, that's what he'd said. So what in God's name had gone wrong? How had we gone from getting better to dead in a matter of hours? *Had my father lied to me?* I wondered. *But why?* I was overwhelmed by sadness and regret. And the guilt, well, like a tsunami it snuck up and then slammed over me.

I knew my father had been admitted and diagnosed with pneumonia the day before. But even though I lived close by—only a few miles from the hospital—I didn't go to see him. It hadn't been that I didn't want to visit. At least I don't think so. I'd called him on Christmas Eve to say I was coming, but he said he was too tired for visitors and not looking his best so I'd let him have his way. I knew how Dad was about being seen when he wasn't looking his best. He never wanted people seeing him—not even his own kids—when his hair wasn't perfectly rolled and coiffed into his famous bouffant style. I'd wanted to respect his wishes.

Or was the real reason I didn't go what my conscience suggested? That it had been convenient for me to let him have his way. It was Christmastime, after all, and I still had cooking and baking and wrapping to do with hardly enough time to get everything finished in time for Christmas morning. Was that really why I had given in to my father's request—and so willingly, at that—when I should have just gone to the hospital to be with him? I was fifteen minutes away, for God's sake. What would it have taken to hop in the car and pop in for a quick visit? I wondered if that's what Dad had been thinking after our phone conversation, when I'd agreed to stay away. Had he complained to Mr. Bobbit after he hung up the phone? I imagined the conversation.

She only lives a few miles away, for God's sake, Mr. Bobbit. Wouldn't you think she'd be here? After all I've done for those kids . . ."

"Well, Mr. Brown, you know how these kids are today."

"I'll let you rest, but I'll be there on Christmas morning," I'd said when I accepted his invitation to stay away. "I won't take no for an answer next time." "OK, baby girl," Dad had replied. It was all a little too easy. Had Dad really been waiting for me to insist on coming? You know parents and their little tests. "Oh no, don't you bother. I know how busy you are, and I'm just fine." When what they really mean is, "Of course I want you here, but you should know that. I shouldn't have to ask." Was Dad testing me? And when I didn't insist on coming, had he watched his hospital door, hoping I'd do the right thing anyway and just show up?

I couldn't bear my own thoughts. My head swirled with "what if" and "if only." What if I'd been with him when his heart stopped? Would he have fought harder to come back? If only I'd known that I'd never again have the chance to say what I'd told him a million times before, but not enough times, that I loved him infinitely and I was so proud he was my father. If only I'd known there would not be another opportunity to say I forgave him for all of the hurt he had caused our family or to ask his forgiveness for the hurt I had caused him. But all the "what ifs" and "if onlys" in the world wouldn't change what was. I had made that terrible human assumption, that there would always be tomorrow to say what needed to be said, to ask for and grant forgiveness, to make amends. Now we had run out of tomorrows.

In the book *For One More Day*, Mitch Albom wrote, "Have you ever lost someone you love and wanted one more conversation, one more chance to make up for the time when you thought they would be here forever? If so, then you know you can go your whole life collecting days, and none will outweigh the one you wish you had back." Why had I been so shortsighted, so selfish? What had made me think Dad would always be around for one more day?

As I sat on the edge of my bed, I wondered if my father had known he was dying. A few hours before he passed, he told Mr. Bobbit, "I'm going away tonight." Mr. Bobbit said he didn't know what to make of it and tossed it off as the fever talking. I asked myself, *Had Dad heard God calling him home? And, if he did, why hadn't he said something to one of us? How sad, I thought, that he'd taken his last breath without the comforting words or the soft touch of someone who loved him.* He should have been surrounded by family when he passed, not people on his payroll. I should have been there with him. I should have insisted on it. But it was past the time for shoulds. I would never have the chance to see my father alive again.

Still, I had to see him.

It was two in the morning, and I looked in on my kids before I headed out to the hospital. Sydney was curled up in a tight little ball under her soft, pink *Beauty and the Beast* comforter and clutched her stuffed horse. Carrington was turned upside down, his head at the foot of his Mickey Mouse bed, his feet on the pillow, and his pajama top with images of fire trucks on it hiked up to the middle of his back. Looking at my sleeping children, I envied them their innocence. As much as I wanted to wake them—to shake them and cry, "Your grandfather is dead! Your grandfather is dead!"—I couldn't. Not on Christmas. Sydney was seven and Carrington was five, and they both still believed in Santa Claus. Their biggest worry that night when I'd tucked them in was whether Santa would find the plate of cookies and glass of milk they'd left for him on the mantelpiece. Broken hearts could wait until morning, after the last presents were unwrapped and after they'd had the chance to see the glass of milk empty and platter of cookies gone.

Trying not to awaken them, I closed the doors to their rooms and padded down to the kitchen to get Christmas dinner started before I left. Standing at the counter, stuffing the giant turkey, I wondered, *Why in God's name am I doing this? Why am I not already in the car and on my way to the hospital? What's so important about preparing the bird when my father is waiting?* I didn't have an answer. At that moment, my head was in a fog, my emotions dull. I dusted the turkey with herbs and spices and slid the roasting pan in the oven, then ran back upstairs, grabbed some clothes, and pulled them on. I didn't even know what I was wearing. Grabbing my car keys, I headed out to the car, hoping I would be able to see well enough through my tears to get to the hospital in one piece. As I backed out of the garage, I heard a loud bang, then a scraping sound. The garbage cans, I thought. I just ran over the garbage cans.

I didn't have time to stop. Putting the car in gear, I drove out of my neighborhood and headed for the hospital. The night was crystal clear but cold for Atlanta, and I shivered against the chill. The road was pretty much all mine—not too many people out at that time—and the trip took less time than I'd expected it would. I felt a strange mix of dread and urgency as I pulled into the hospital parking lot. My anxiety heightened as I rode the elevator up to Dad's floor. The elevator doors rattled open and the nurse at the desk looked up. "Can I help you?" she asked. "My father is James Brown," I said. The nurse smiled a sad little smile, got up from her chair, and led me to Dad's room. I walked inside, closing the door behind me. Dad looked so peaceful, as if he were soundly sleeping. For years he'd been complaining about how tired he was. I dropped

5

down beside him and took his hand in mine. It was still warm. "You can finally get some rest, Dad," I said, laying my head on his chest. I inhaled deeply, taking in his familiar scent. He smelled the way he always did, clean and outdoorsy, like his favorite fragrance, "Lauren." I remembered how once I'd pointed out to him that it was a woman's perfume and how he'd shrugged and said, "Doesn't matter to me, Yamma. I like how it smells."

I closed my eyes and memories washed over me. So many memories. I remembered Dad sitting with my older sister, Deanna, and me in the den of our home in Beech Island, South Carolina, his hair rolled in huge, pastel-colored curlers, telling us stories from his past, the same stories, over and over again. Stories other people would pay to hear, and we, as his children, took for granted. Each time he started one, Deanna and I would roll our eyes as if to say, *Oh no, not again!* He told us about how he'd helped prevent rioting after Dr. Martin Luther King's assassination with a televised concert that calmed people down. He talked about visiting President Lyndon Johnson in the White House, and how proud he was when *Look* magazine put his picture on its cover and asked: "Is this the Most Important Black Man in America?" "And I was!" he said, his chest puffed out with pride every time he told the story.

He told us about visiting President Richard Nixon and lecturing him on race issues. They liked each other, odd couple that they were. Dad played at Nixon's 1969 inauguration and then endorsed him for a second term four years later, even though he knew it wouldn't be a popular move with many of his fans. Dad didn't give a rat's ass. He was too imperious to care. He was James Brown, a celebrity among presidents and superstars. I thought about the time Denzel Washington came backstage and how proud I felt when I saw that Denzel was starstruck meeting my dad (but Dad was unfazed!), and I recalled those times when Dad would pick me up, tuck me into the back seat of our big, black van and then drive for miles on dirt roads for his favorite foot-long chili dogs. Sometimes he'd have two. I never let on that I hated them.

I had so many sweet memories of Dad, but there had been plenty of sadness, too. Until I was grown, every time I heard him raise his voice, even when he was talking business on the phone, I shook with fear. I had heard that rage so many times as a child, and it usually meant he was high and pummeling Mom behind closed doors. I was just seven when, a few days after one of those beatings, Mom picked up Deanna and me at a Halloween party at a neighbor's and, instead of heading home, drove all the way from Beech Island to Washington, DC, where our grandmother lived. She was finished with the abuse. After that, Deanna and I spent only summers in South Carolina. When Dad was on the road, we were left in the care of the housekeeper, a kindly woman named Miss Ella, who had as much to do with raising us as our parents did. When Miss Ella wasn't around, we were usually watched by one of Dad's girlfriends, and they were all pretty strange.

Holding Dad's hand and remembering those times, my mind turned to thoughts of his companion. Her name was Tomi Rae Hynie, and she was a real doozy. The last I'd heard she was in rehab somewhere in California for what she'd said was an addiction to prescription drugs. I wondered if she even knew Dad died. *Had Mr. Bobbit called her?* I wondered. It wasn't my job to tell her. Tomi Rae was nothing if not a drama queen, and I didn't have it in me to deal with her right then. I just wanted to spend as much time with my father as I possibly could before I would never be able to see his face or touch his skin again.

I stayed in that hospital room for what seemed like a long time, a daughter stealing a few final moments alone with her father, the scenes from our times together playing over and over in my head.

As so often happens when a loved one passes, I chose to let the bad times fade away, at least for those last few minutes of holding onto him. I didn't want to let go, so I held on even tighter. I was grateful that nobody bothered us, that nobody tried to hurry me out of the room. I may have been thinking that if I stayed just a few minutes longer, my father would eventually open his eyes and I would tell him about the things I had been thinking about while he was asleep.

I prayed hard for divine intervention. *Please God, let this be a colossal mistake. Wait! Was that a heartbeat I heard? Did Dad's eyes flutter open for just a split second? Did I feel his breath on my cheek?* I tried to shake off the tricks my mind was playing on me. I couldn't accept that my father's heart was no longer beating, that blood no longer coursed through his veins, that, after nearly forty years of having a father, I no longer did. My father was dead. There would be no miracle, not that day, not for Dad and me. I asked him questions anyway. "Did you really love me, Dad? Why was it so easy for you to walk away?" I told him what I should have when I knew he could hear me. "I understand, Dad. You did the best you could. No one ever taught you how to love. I'm sorry for that. I'm sorry for you, and I'm sorry for me."

I don't know how much time passed when it finally dawned on me that I could sit there at his beside for an eternity and it wouldn't make any difference. My beloved father was gone. And I had to tell my family. As I stood to leave, the glint of his silver bicycle chain bracelet caught my eye. It didn't seem like his style, but he wore it all the time. I gently removed it from his wrist and placed it on mine, an inexpensive but priceless symbol linking me to him even in death. I still wear it every day.

I have never felt as alone as I did walking out of that hospital room. I knew Dad was dead, but I couldn't *believe* he was gone. I stood in the hallway and tried to stifle my grief, but it was no use. I slid down the wall into a heap on the floor and sobbed. "It was a fine cry—loud and long—but it had no bottom and it had no top, just circles and circles of sorrow," Toni Morrison wrote in *Sula*. Yes, that was it. My grief was infinite, with no bottom and no top, "just circles and circles of sorrow." That was it exactly.

I thought of my sister. She was especially close to Dad, and she was going to take his death really hard. Deanna was somewhere in Mexico on vacation, and I had no idea where she was staying or how to get in touch with her. But I had to try to find her. I hoped that she'd mentioned the name of the hotel to one of her friends. I'd have to try to find phone numbers for the names of the friends I knew. I didn't want Deanna to get the news from someone else, some talking head on CNN or the BBC. It wouldn't be long before the story was carried around the globe. The press had already begun gathering outside the hospital, which gave me a strange sense of pride, knowing that reporters and photographers from all over the world would record the event. Yes, the death of a music legend was an event. There was no way around it. James Brown, the Godfather of Soul, had millions of fans, and they deserved to know that he was gone.

Mr. Bobbit found me and informed me that a press conference had already been arranged. Did I want to speak? *Really?* I get that business is business, but I thought it was an odd request. I had just lost my Dad, and he was asking me to face a group of strangers looking for a sound bite—even before I'd had a chance to talk to the rest of my family. Why couldn't Dad's "people" ever separate the celebrity from the man? I immediately switched from the grieving daughter to the take-charge woman I had to be. No, I told Mr. Bobbit, I didn't want to talk to a group of reporters. Wasn't that what he and the lawyers and the publicist and everyone else Dad had employed to spin James Brown were paid the big bucks to do? All I cared about was getting my father's body out of there before someone from the *National Enquirer* had the chance to sneak in the hospital and take a picture of him on his deathbed. And I needed to get in touch with my family members before they got the news from a reporter.

While I made the arrangements to have Dad's body taken back home to Augusta, Mr. Bobbit and Joel Katz, my father's lawyer, talked to the reporters. They told them Dad's premonition about his own death and described his final moments in more detail than I would have liked. "He sat bolt upright in his hospital bed, grasped his chest, and yelled, 'I'm on fire! I'm on fire,'" Mr. Bobbit said. A few minutes later, he said, my father sighed three times, then closed his eyes and died. I was haunted by the image of Dad passing without a loved one there to support him. Why couldn't the last face he saw before he took his final breath have been mine rather than a paid employee? I felt sick and ashamed.

The sun was rising when I finally left the hospital and headed back home, confident that our family friend, Charlie Reid, a funeral director from Augusta, would handle the transportation of Dad's body from the hospital to the funeral home and that the hospital security staff would make sure no one got into the room before Mr. Reid arrived. At that point, I was so riddled with grief and guilt that I wasn't even aware of the drive across town. One minute I was pulling out of the hospital parking lot, and the next minute I was in my driveway, negotiating the garage through the tears clouding my eyes.

I barely had time to get in the house when my cell phone rang. David Cannon, Dad's accountant and business manager, was calling. Cannon said he needed to discuss some business deals that Dad hadn't had a chance to sign off on before he died. I could hardly believe his insensitivity. My father wasn't even gone two hours, and his friends were focused on press conferences and business deals. Who does that? What was *wrong* with these people? "Call me later," I said brusquely. Then I went to the kitchen to tend to my turkey and wait for Darren and the kids to wake up to celebrate Christmas.

I knew they'd be up at the crack of dawn, and sure enough, they were. The sun wasn't even completely up when the kids came tearing down the stairs, screaming, "Santa was here! Santa was here! Look at all these packages!" As they ripped through their presents, I did my best to try to seem happy and engaged. With the kids preoccupied with their gifts, Darren tried talking about Dad's estate and what came next and who might get what, but I waved him off. When I felt myself cracking, I went upstairs to my room and turned on the TV to block out the sound of my sobs.

Deanna arrived at my house late that afternoon, wiping away tears with a handful of tissues. Just as I'd feared, she'd heard the news on CNN and caught the next flight back from Mexico. She looked dog-tired. We hugged for a long time and then got down to business. Our time to digest our father's death was finished whether we were ready or not. There was so much to do in such a short time.

By then, Dad's body was on the way to Augusta, thanks to Mr. Reid, and the phone was ringing nonstop with calls from reporters (*How did they get our cell phone numbers?* I wondered) and family members and friends. Through the numbness of our grief, Deanna and I attempted to navigate our way from one step to the next between taking calls. We weren't just planning a funeral for our father. We were organizing the public farewell for an American music icon. Thousands and thousands of people would want to pay their respects to the Godfather, and we knew Dad would want that.

At least we didn't go hungry as we sat at my kitchen table, sketching out plans. I had cooked up a storm to keep myself from falling apart. Turkey. Ham. Macaroni and cheese. Collard greens. String beans. Even sweet potato pie. There's a reason they call it comfort food, and we all dug in as if it were our last meal. By the end of the night we had planned three services, two public and one private. But the real work—and the real grief—was just beginning.

Deanna and I got up early the next morning and made the two and a half hour drive from Atlanta to Beech Island, South Carolina, just across the Savannah River from Augusta, where she and my father lived only a few miles apart. Dad had kept the house where I'd spent a good part of my early childhood, although it had been added on to and redecorated several times since then. Between needing permission from lawyers and managers and estate trustees, we knew it would practically take an act of Congress to get past the guardhouse of his place, but we finally got in.

We brought a video camera to record the inside of the house, as it was the last time Dad was there. When I saw the unfinished bowl of cereal sitting on the kitchen counter, right where he left it the last time he was there, I lost it. The cereal was soggy and the milk spoiled, but I held the bowl in both of my hands as if it were sacred. And to me, it was. My father had touched that bowl, eaten from it, just days earlier, when everything was still "normal." I'm sure when he went to his dentist that day, he expected that he'd be back by dinnertime. But the dentist, concerned about Dad's appearance, had sent him to the ER and he'd never come home. Life can be so cruelly unpredictable.

Deanna and I decided that Dad would be dressed in different outfits for each of the three services. Our main reason for being at his home was to choose what he would wear. His walk-in closet was jam-packed with stage costumes. At first, I felt awkward about going through his things. Dad was a private man and funny about who came into his bedroom. Even though as a child I had been in the room countless times, without him there I somehow felt as if we were being intrusive. But my overwhelming sense of duty to him won out over my discomfort, and we went to work at the task at hand. Dad was all about showmanship. It was my duty to make sure his fans saw him in his finest clothes. Well, that closet must have had every custom-made outfit that Dad had ever performed in. There were racks of jackets with sparkles and matching shirts and slacks. Rows of custom boots: leather, sequined, patent leather. And bow ties. Did I mention that he had hundreds? Deanna and I couldn't believe our eyes.

As we went about the task of choosing his clothing, we were getting calls from reporters about Dad's then-wife (or companion, I'm still not sure which she was) Tomi Rae. She didn't disappoint. She'd left rehab in California and come back to Beech Island armed with plenty of drama. The day before, as cameras whirled and clicked, she'd kneeled outside the padlocked gate leading to the estate and cried to reporters about being barred from her own home. It was a picture seen around the world, and it was embarrassing for everyone.

Dad had appointed three trustees to oversee his estate: his attorney, Buddy Dallas; a former judge and longtime acquaintance, Al Bradley; and David Cannon. It was true the trustees had barred Tomi Rae from the property. They claimed she didn't have the right to be there unless she could prove she was my father's wife. The issue arose because Tomi Rae had been married previously and the trustees claimed she wasn't legally divorced in 2001 when she married Dad. Her side of the story was that the previous marriage had been annulled before she and my father took their wedding vows. We didn't know what the truth was and, at that point, we didn't care. There was too much work to be done. But television, news-papers, and *People* magazine all played up the saga of the grieving widow, bundled up in a coat and scarf, her gloved hands clutching the wrought iron gates, crying that she and the son she had with Dad, five-year-old James Jr., had no money and nowhere to go.

It had somehow gotten back to Deanna and me that Tomi Rae thought we were responsible for isolating her, and, even though we weren't, the stage for a media circus had been set. I wouldn't have expected anything less from her. It's not as if everyone was form-ing a united front against poor Tomi Rae. We were having our own issues with the trustees. They were tightfisted and uncommunica-tive. They controlled Dad's accounts but contributed nothing to the funeral plans and questioned everything from the flowers to the casket. "Did he really need a casket made of gold?" they wondered. *Are you serious?* Here was a man who always wanted the best for him-self, a showman who had worked himself out of poverty and took great pride in his success, and these men had the audacity to ask if a gold casket was *necessary?* Besides, it was *his money* they were talking about, not theirs. Damn them! How dare they question our choice of casket. They may have worked for him, but we were his family.

We ended up pooling our resources and paying for it ourselves.

2

Three Funerals and Michael Jackson

"He who has gone, so we but cherish his memory, abides with us, more potent, nay, more present than the living man."
—Antoine de Saint-Exupéry

THE FIRST OF the three funeral services over as many days was held at the Apollo Theater in Harlem, where Dad had gotten his start in the entertainment business. We wanted the service to be as spectacular as his shows were, complete with costume changes and the 24-carat-gold-plated casket. Just when we thought that every last detail had been worked out, Mr. Reid called to inform us that the casket we had chosen was too heavy to transport by private plane and the last commercial flight that could get Dad to New York in time for the viewing had already left Augusta. Now that was a fine mess. Fans were already lining up outside the Apollo, jockeying for position for a final glimpse of the Godfather of Soul, and he had missed the last flight that could get him there. I could see the headline in the New York tabloids: GODFATHER OF SOUL A NO-SHOW AT HIS OWN FUNERAL. Deanna and I were beside ourselves with worry. "What are we going to do?" I asked. "Whatever it takes to get him there," my sister replied.

My father lived by the rule "the show must go on." He could be sick as a dog, but he still showed up and rocked the house because he never wanted to disappoint his fans. "When I'm on stage, I'm trying to do one thing: bring people joy," he once said. "Just like church does. People don't go to church to find trouble. They go there to lose it." We had to do right by Dad. He would be horrified to know that his final show, on his favorite stage, for his most loyal fans, was about to be canceled because his kids had picked a casket that couldn't fly. I prayed to God for an answer, and Rev. Al Sharpton appeared.

Dad had been a mentor and father figure to Rev. Sharpton going back to the early 1970s. Rev. Sharpton was barely twenty when they met, but he was already a street preacher and the leader of a civil rights organization for black youth. Shortly after they met my father's firstborn, Teddy, from his first marriage, to Velma Warren, died tragically in a car crash at nineteen years old. Rev. Sharpton became a sort of replacement son. My Dad loved Rev. Sharpton, and Rev. Sharpton said it was my father who taught him to be a man. I know Dad introduced him to his pompadour hairstyle and his former wife, Kathy Jordan, a backup singer in the band. When Rev. Sharpton heard about our casket predicament, he charged to the rescue. If Mr. Reid was willing to drive the hearse to New York, he said—Rev. Sharpton doesn't drive—he was willing to keep him company and keep him awake for the eight-hundred-mile drive. And that's what they did. Rounding up a group of pallbearers after dinner on that Wednesday, December 27, 2006, they loaded Dad's golden casket into the hearse in

Augusta and drove all night, arriving in Harlem thirteen hours later, at midmorning on Thursday, in the nick of time for the public viewing. I still chuckle at picturing them pulling up to a traffic light somewhere in the Deep South and the people in the next car looking over at the hearse and seeing Rev. Sharpton. *Martha, you ain't gonna believe who I just saw* . . .

Rev. Sharpton took charge of the New York City viewing. He made sure that the pageantry of the day was befitting the Godfather of Soul. Just after noon, a glass carriage, pulled by two colossal white horses wearing feather plumes on their heads, carried my father's body from Rev. Sharpton's office the twenty or so blocks to the historic Apollo. Dad loved performing there, and he always packed them in. But I was still stunned to see the crowds that had gathered in Harlem. It was December, yet some fans had waited overnight in the freezing cold for the chance to pay their respects. Rows of people standing ten deep chanted, "James Brown, James Brown, James Brown," as the carriage carrying the gleaming casket made its way down Malcolm X Boulevard toward the theater on 125th Street. The atmosphere along the procession route was downright festive. Dad's music blared from local businesses and people sang and danced in the streets. Some people carried signs. RIP GODFATHER. I FEEL GOOD THAT YOU'RE HOME WITH US, BROTHER BROWN. WE LOVE YOU, JAMES BROWN. PAPA WILL BE MISSED!

At the Apollo, the marquee read "REST IN PEACE APOLLO LEGEND/THE GODFATHER OF SOUL/JAMES BROWN/1933–2006." When the carriage stopped in front of the theater, hundreds of people, some of them clutching pictures of my father, whooped and cheered. It was quite a spectacle; Dad would have loved that even in death he could fire up a crowd. The pallbearers carried the casket from the carriage into the theater and up onto the stage, setting it down in the precise spot where Dad had performed his *Live at the Apollo* album more than four decades earlier. Taking it all in, I could almost hear the drumroll and prelude of Fats Gonder, the emcee who had introduced Dad dozens of times over his career: *So now, ladies and gentlemen, it is star time. Are you ready for star time? Thank you, and thank you very kindly. It is indeed a great pleasure to present to you at this particular time, nationally and internationally known as the Hardest Working Man in Show Business . . . Mr. Please Please Please himself. The star of the show, James Brown!* Would I ever stop crying? Would life ever seem normal again?

The lid on the casket was lifted and the seven-hour viewing began. Dad looked fine in his glittery blue suit with silver trim and epaulets and matching silver shoes. The flashy blue suit would be used for the Apollo viewing because it reminded us of the times he performed there with his backup singers, the Famous Flames. He often said those were some of the best moments of his life. The affair was classic James Brown, outsized and over the top. The theater was jammed—standing room only—and for several hours, while his music blared in the background, fans walked single-file past the open casket to pay homage to the Godfather of Soul. The energy in that room felt physical and it was exhausting beyond anything I had ever experienced before. All of those people had taken time out of their lives to honor my father. It was mind-blowing. Outside, lines of people snaked around the building, waiting for the chance to get in. Deanna and I wanted to greet as many fans as we could, so, with Rev. Sharpton accompanying us, we walked outside and made our way down the line on 125th Street, thanking people for coming. Working the crowd, we really felt the love.

By the time we left Harlem that night to head for the airport for the return trip to Augusta, I was numb with fatigue. But there was still too much to do to surrender to sleep. We arrived at Deanna's at around two that Friday morning and immediately began going through pictures and putting the finishing touches on the eulogy for the hometown public viewing, which was to take place at the James Brown Arena in Augusta on Saturday. Meanwhile, the private, family funeral was just hours away. When I finally fell into bed, I tossed and turned, worrying about the private service and the potential for disaster. Dad was married four times and he had seven kids from those marriages (his son Teddy, from his first marriage, had died in a car crash years earlier). The posturing and BS over his estate and where he should be buried had already begun. Almost immediately, the family divided into camps, and everyone had an opinion. Then there was the Tomi Rae drama. It didn't help that we listed her in the private funeral program as Dad's companion and not his wife or that Rev. Sharpton got her name wrong and called her Tammy. (That may have been done deliberately, just to get under her skin. It worked.)

The private funeral was held at the Carpentersville Baptist Church in North Augusta, my sister's church. The tiny brick church spilled over with mourners, three hundred of our closest family and friends jammed inside for a standing room only service. The only famous faces were boxing promoter Don King, rapper MC Hammer, and comedian Dick Gregory. It was a humble affair compared to the first public service at the Apollo the day before or the second to follow in Augusta a day later, but I have to say that in many ways it was my favorite. It was an old-fashioned church revival. There were plenty of prayers and gospel music sung by the church choir. At times, it was raucous, with people clapping and dancing and cheering—the way it always is at a Baptist service. It was long and loud and everyone got his or her praise on. One of the most moving moments for me was when the choir sang Dad's favorite hymn, "His Eye Is on the Sparrow":

I sing because I'm happy,
I sing because I'm free,
For His eye is on the sparrow,
And I know He watches me.

Tomi Rae did her best to avoid any eye contact with us, and we did the same. It wasn't always easy to ignore her, especially when she wailed louder than anyone else, pushed her way up on the stage, and even fainted a couple of times. I sensed she had an attitude toward my sister and me, too. I know she felt slighted because people paid more attention to us than her, but we were his kids, and many of them had known us since we were little girls. I'd be lying if I said I didn't enjoy the fact that we were in charge and Tomi Rae was on the outside looking in. That's how I had often felt around Dad's lovers—like an outsider. His focus was always on *them*. Tomi Rae had been the last in the long string of his women, and she had been in his life for only a few years, on and off. Theirs had been one heck of a tumultuous affair (always was with Dad). I know her wish to be at the center of attention got the best of Rev. Sharpton, and he made it known again during his eulogy. "If you really are all that you say you are, you don't place yourself in the story. The story puts you in your place," he said, glancing at the front row where Tomi Rae sat with young James. "We don't want to hear your story or your mess. We're here because of James Brown." Then he asked her to move back to the second row because the first was reserved for family. I have to admit I felt myself slink down in the pew.

When the service was over and I dragged myself to the car to go back to my sister's house, I couldn't help but be relieved there was only one more to go. I was physically and emotionally beyond exhausted. All I wanted was a glass of wine and some quiet time. Darren and I were staying with Deanna and her husband, Shawn.

That night, we were all just about to turn in when the phone rang. It was past midnight and we couldn't imagine who would be calling so late. Deanna answered the phone. Mr. Reid was on the line. "Sorry to be calling so late," he said, "but Michael Jackson just called. He's in town and he wants to come over to the funeral home and sit with your father."

Deanna repeated his words to me and we looked at each other, incredulous. The King of Pop had been MIA since the year before, when he'd moved to the Middle East after his acquittal on child molestation charges. Now he was in Augusta? Mr. Reid explained that Michael had returned to the United States under the cover of darkness for the sole purpose of paying his respects to my father. I looked at Deanna and knew she was thinking what I was. If anyone found out that Michael Jackson was in town, there would be bedlam in our tranquil little city—and Dad would be upstaged at his hometown send-off.

"When does he want to come?" I asked.

Deanna posed the question to Mr. Reid.

"Now," he said.

"But it's—"

"I know," Mr. Reid replied.

After days of refereeing the family squabbles that had already begun over Dad's estate and of sharing my grief publicly with legions of his fans, all I wanted was for all the hoopla to end so my father could be laid to rest and I could mourn in private. But who turned away the world's most famous entertainer and after he had traveled nearly eight thousand miles from another continent to be there? It wasn't going to be Deanna and me. Besides, my father adored Michael, loved him like a son. Thinking back to that bizarre night, I am reminded of one of Dad's stories.

When Elvis Presley died in August 1977, Dad dropped everything and chartered a private plane to go to him that very same day. I was only five at the time, so I don't remember the details of him leaving us. But the way he told it, Elvis's death hit a little too close to home, and Dad felt as if he had to get to Memphis right away to be with his friend. The crowds were already gathered at Graceland by the time Dad got there, so he was whisked into the compound through a side gate, in a car driven by an agent from the Tennessee Bureau of Investigation. Ah, the perks of superstardom. After paying his condolences to Priscilla and little Lisa Marie, Dad walked over to Elvis's open casket, which was at the far end of the living room, and broke down. "You rat," he cried in his squeaky voice, sobbing over Elvis's corpse. "Why did you leave me? How could you let it go? How *could* you let it go?" Dad and Elvis inhabited a different stratosphere than the rest of the world. They lived at the pinnacle of celebrity, a lonely, cynical place that people don't truly understand unless they've been there—and those people are a precious few. When Dad lost Elvis, he lost more than a friend. He lost a trusted comrade. Elvis didn't need Dad or judge him or have some hidden agenda. He was someone who understood Dad's crazy, cloistered world.

So it was with Michael and my father. Michael once said in an interview with Oprah Winfrey that when he was five or six years old and living in Indiana, his mother would awaken him at night when Dad was on TV so he could watch him dance. Michael was awestruck by Dad's leaps, splits, and slides. "I used to get angry at the cameraman because whenever he would really start to dance they would be on a close-up so I couldn't see his feet," he told Oprah. "I'd shout, 'Show him! Show him!' so I could watch and learn." Oprah asked, "So he was a big mentor for you?" "Phenomenal," Michael replied in his high-pitched voice, smiling and shaking his head from side to side. "Phenomenal."

Michael often said Dad inspired his music career, and after the Jackson Five became famous and they got to know each other, Dad played the role of a kind of surrogate father to Michael, guiding him, encouraging him, accepting him for the unique person he was. With Dad gone, Michael had lost one of the few people in the world he trusted. Dad's death was personal. *Why did you leave me? How could you let it go?* I understood his need to see my father, even if it was in a dark, lonely funeral parlor in the wee hours of the morning.

Imagine this scene: the King of Pop, arriving at a funeral home in Augusta in the middle of the night, flanked by a dozen of his Nation of Islam bodyguards in their black suits and red bowties and no one there to see it. I didn't either. I was reminded of the philosophical riddle, "if a tree falls in a forest . . ." But Mr. Reid witnessed the whole thing and afterward gave us a blow-by-blow account of what happened.

Michael was wearing a scarf over his head when he and his brigade strode into the funeral home at half past midnight. He took a moment to pray in the chapel and then strode to the room where my father lay in repose. The lid of the casket was up, and Michael bent over and kissed Dad. Staring down at him and caressing his cheek, he told Mr. Reid how much he loved my father and how much Dad had inspired him. At one point, Michael twisted a piece of Dad's hair around his finger and placed the curl on Dad's forehead, just the way my father had so often worn it during performances. I thought that was kind of strange but also kind of sweet. For the next hour or so, caressing Dad's hair as he spoke, Michael peppered Mr. Reid with questions. Odd questions.

"What types of fluids do you use?" he asked.

"How do you style the hair of a corpse?"

"Are you going to change his outfit before the morning service?"

"Who chose the casket?"

"Is it what Mr. Brown would have wanted?"

Mr. Reid called us right after Michael left. He told us that while Michael was in the funeral parlor, he had asked to see the casket room. He had taken his time there, studying the different models on display. Mr. Reid said that it almost seemed as if he were contemplating his own death. Looking back now, it was downright prophetic. When Michael returned to Dad's side, he asked one of his bodyguards to take a picture of them together. The camera flashed, and they all went on their way.

I had just gotten to sleep again when Mr. Reid called for the third time that night. Deanna came into the room and shook me awake.

"You won't believe this," she said. "Mr. Reid is on the phone again and he says Michael wants to go back to the funeral home."

She was right. I couldn't believe it. Michael told Mr. Reid that there were things he had wanted to say to Dad but felt he couldn't with his bodyguards present. He wanted to come back and spend time alone with Dad. What could we say?

"Uh, OK."

As Mr. Reid would tell it, a few minutes later, the brigade of big black SUVs snaked back up the driveway to the front of the funeral parlor for the second time that night. This time when the engines stopped, only Michael emerged. He strode back into the funeral home and thanked Mr. Reid for having him again. Mr. Reid set a chair next to the casket and told Michael to stay as long as he liked. He stayed for five hours, finally leaving at dawn. I had to wonder what went on in that room. What had Michael said to Dad when it was just the two of them? What was he was thinking as he sat there, staring into that casket?

We never expected Michael to show up at the public service later that day. We later learned he hadn't planned on attending, but Rev. Sharpton convinced him to stay. Michael hadn't made a public appearance in the year and a half since he'd left the country. He was greeted with a thunderous roar as he slipped into the James Brown Arena that afternoon. At first I didn't know what was happening. Then I saw the shimmering black hair bobbing over the heads of the people seated up front. Michael, dressed in a black jacket and pants with a white shirt, a thin black tie, and dark glasses, quietly took a seat near the front. I was surprised at how rail thin he looked in person. He was completely unassuming, even shy. I knew how hard it must have been for him to be there. The arena (which had been the Augusta Arena until it was renamed for Dad four months before he passed) was a full house, with eight thousand–plus people. Michael, of course, completely eclipsed the constellation of stars present.

Once again, Rev. Sharpton presided over the service, with Rev. Jesse Jackson at his side. Dad's former band members Bootsy Collins and Bobby Byrd were there, as was Danny Ray, whose job it was to announce Dad before performances and wrap him in his trademark cape when he collapsed in mock exhaustion onstage. We had obviously chosen well from Dad's closet for his final appearance. The next day, the *New York Times* wrote about what they called his "hallmark pomp. He wore a black suit with sequined lapels, a fire-engine red shirt, a black bowtie, black gloves and a pair of black shoes tipped with yet more sequins." I could almost hear Dad saying, "Good job, girls."

The final service lasted all afternoon. The bleachers were jammed. A video of Dad's last performance, in London, was projected on a huge overhead screen, and his music blared throughout the arena. Mr. Bobbit eulogized Dad with a story about that last night in the hospital.

"I slept in his room that night," Mr. Bobbit said. "He wanted lemonade. He wanted water. He wanted his feet rubbed. He wanted this; he wanted that. But he didn't want to talk to anyone. He didn't want to see anyone. . . . He slept from Saturday afternoon until Christmas morning. About 1:15 he said, 'Mr. Bobbit, I'm burning up, and my chest is on fire.' I gave him some water, a wet cloth, put it on his forehead and that. So he would lay down, sit up, lay down, sit up, lay down, sit up.

"Before then, about a week ago, he said, 'Mr. Bobbit, I asked God to give you and me twenty more years.' I said, 'Mr. Brown, I'm seventy-six years old. I don't think I can handle twenty. Maybe you can.' He said, 'No, man, no, they can make us young; we'll be around for a long time. We're going to do things with Michael Jackson. We're going to do things with Prince and do this, do that.' I said, 'OK, Mr. Brown.' Because you didn't say no to Mr. Brown. You might say maybe, but you didn't say no. So, anyway, he laid there, [and] he said, 'Mr. Bobbit, I'm going to leave here tonight.' . . . And I wanted to cheer him up. And I said, 'Well, and if you're saying what I think you're saying, I can't make this trip with you.' So we kind of laughed.

"He sat on the foot of the bed. He made his peace with his God. He laid back. He laid his head back on the bed and he exposed himself by laying back. And I took a blanket and I covered over him. And that's how I was able to hear him breathe his last three sighs. He breathed very softly three times. He opened his eyes. He closed his eyes. And he had expired. I called the nurses and the doctors. They came. They worked on him for a long time, but he was gone."

What a tender story. I wished it had been mine. Everywhere I looked, people choked back tears. I glanced over at Michael and could see he was genuinely grief stricken. His famously tarnished face was twisted in sadness. When someone tried to goad him into performing on stage, he politely demurred. I had never met Michael before that day, and under normal circumstances, I would have been completely starstruck. But this was my father's funeral, the third in as many days, and I was drained. By then, God could have walked in and I wouldn't have reacted.

Rev. Sharpton was sensitive to Michael's position. Before calling him up to stand onstage, he delivered a rousing endorsement of the King of Pop. He told about his last conversation with Dad and how Dad had asked about Michael. "Even though [Michael] knew they were going to criticize him, Michael came for you today, Mr. Brown," Rev. Sharpton said. "I don't care what the media says. James Brown wanted Michael Jackson with him here today." The crowd roared.

As the band played Dad's music and Michael stirred the crowd with kind words about the man he called his "greatest inspiration," the magnitude of Dad's death really hit me. I looked at him, lying in that gold-plated casket, knowing it would be the last time I ever saw him.

And I wondered, *What am I going to do without you?*

3

Walton Way

"The ultimate measure of a man is not where he stands in moments of comfort and convenience, but where he stands at times of challenge and controversy."

—*Martin Luther King Jr.*

OUR FIRST HOUSE was in a ritzy residential area of Augusta, on a street called Walton Way. Our neighbors were Augusta's aristocracy: doctors and lawyers and other high-powered professionals. You could hardly miss us. We were the only African American family, and we had a pony in the backyard. At Christmastime, the glowing, blinking black Santa Claus on the front lawn gave us away. Dad had our animated Santa custom-made along with Uncle Sam and Frosty the Snowman and a host of other illuminated cartoon figures. Every year, a new character popped up. And every year, from Thanksgiving to New Year's Day, curiosity seekers came from all over to see our Christmas pageant. I remember peeking out from behind our heavy living room curtains and seeing cars creeping past our house, most of them stopping just long enough for the people inside to ogle the twinkling, jerking display and snap a few photographs before driving off. I'm not sure if they came for the decorations or for a glimpse of James Brown changing a dead bulb or righting a leaning lawn ornament. It was probably a little of both.

Walton Way is ten minutes and a pipe dream from the hot, swarming district of Augusta where Dad spent most of his childhood. He went to live there, in his aunt Honey's whorehouse, when he wasn't quite six years old. The neighborhood was called the Terry, short for Negro Territory, and it was a step up from where he had lived before with his father in a series of tar paper huts in the dense pinewoods of Barnwell, South Carolina, about an hour's drive southeast of Augusta. Dad's mother left when he was four, and he spent a lot of time alone in the woods while his father went looking for work at the turpentine camps in Georgia and Florida. Occasionally, he was left in the care of one of the women his father brought around, but they never stayed around for very long. I look at my own kids and try to imagine them, at four and five years old, living in a desolate shack with no electricity or running water, making their own meals, going to sleep all alone, with no one there when they awakened in the middle of the night to a thunderstorm or from a bad dream or with a stomachache. Dad must have been frightened a lot and terribly lonesome. I remember he said he played with sticks and sang songs to pass the time. He was five when his father gave him a harmonica, and that became his comfort and his best friend. Being alone so much at such a young age had a profound effect on my father. He would often say it gave him "his own mind." It showed him he didn't need anybody. Maybe so, but I think those early years kindled a deep sadness and the explosive rage he would carry to the end of his life.

Of course, life at Aunt Honey's had its own challenges.

Augusta is best known for the Masters Golf Tournament, which is held every year on the pristine fairways of the Augusta National Golf Club, a few miles from Walton Way. The club was built on the grounds of a former slave plantation in 1933, the same year Dad was born, and for decades it was a bastion of southern blue bloods and all-white golf. It wasn't until 1990, when I was in college, that the club invited its first black member to join, and that was under extreme pressure from the outside world. (It took until 2012 for them to accept women as members.)

When Dad's father brought him to live in the Terry in 1938, he knew nothing about the lives of the rich white men behind the gates of Augusta National, the same privileged class of people who would one day be his neighbors on Walton Way. In the Terry, the streets were made of red clay and sand and had names like Thank God Alley and Slopjar Alley. The Ku Klux Klan sometimes paraded down the main drag.

Dad loved telling stories about living in the Terry. As he told it, Aunt Honey's brothel on Twiggs Street was one of the main attractions there. Most of the other homes were unpainted shanties, but Aunt Honey's place had paint, as well as two floors and lots of rooms that were always full. There was always something going on there, and it was usually illegal. Besides prostitution, there was gambling and plenty of homemade moonshine and enough hog jowls and potato pones and chitlins to feed anyone in the neighborhood who was hungry.

I know that even as an adult Dad hated being alone, which is why he always had a woman and a backup companion. At Aunt Honey's there were always people coming and going. Lots of folks showed up at mealtime, and Aunt Honey fed them all. There were unemployed farm workers, young mothers and their children who lived in the alley behind the brothel, and soldiers who walked in from off the streets. It didn't matter who they were or how much trouble they were in. They were always welcome at Aunt Honey's table. But when the police showed up with the paddy wagon, which happened every few months, everyone scattered.

Dad shined shoes to help earn his keep at Aunt Honey's. Sundays were his best days. Augusta had a saying back then that there was a church for every liquor store in town, and Dad hit all of them. He shined shoes until his knuckles bled, a nickel a shine, and sometimes earned enough on a single Sunday to pay Aunt Honey's monthly rent. The Hardest Working Man in Show Business had been the hardest working kid in the Terry.

Some "bad cats," as my father called them, hung out at Aunt Honey's, and he tried to stay out of their way. He used to tell the story of one man who was particularly mean to him. Once, he said, the man stripped him naked, tied him up in a burlap sack, and beat him until he lost consciousness. That was one story he was willing to tell. I can't help but wonder how many others he either kept secret or forced himself to forget.

Dad's father wasn't around much to protect him, and when he did show up, he was usually angry and ranting about what some white person had done to him. Those rants had a real effect on Dad. What bothered him was that his father cursed white people in private, calling them crackers and worse, but he was submissive in their presence and addressed them as "Yessir" and "Nawsir," even when they were ill-mannered and condescending. Dad called such behavior acting like a "boy," and he vowed never to compromise his own self-respect the way his father had. As a man, my father addressed his friends and acquaintances, black and white, with a "Mr." preceding their last names, and he taught us to do the same. He insisted on being treated with the same respect. People in the

Terry called Dad "Little Junior." On Walton Way, no matter who you were, or how much money you made, he was Mr. Brown.

Dad left the South for a while after he became famous. He had been living in New York for more than a decade when my mom convinced him to move back to his roots, because she believed that the South was a better place to raise children. My sister Deanna was three and I was about to be born when they bought the house on Walton Way. Just recently, we were reminiscing about the old neighborhood, and Deanna told me that she still doesn't know of any black families living there. If that's true, it's astonishing—almost as astonishing as a black man owning a home on Walton Way in the early 1970s.

Dad was keenly aware that his celebrity status opened doors, even in some of the most unlikely places, and he took advantage of that to push his political agenda. He was definitely not anti-white—his accountant and two of his four wives were white—but his commitment to racial equality was second only to his dedication to his music career. His 1968 hit song "Say It Loud—I'm Black and I'm Proud" speaks for itself: "I've worked on jobs with my feet and my hands / But all the work I did was for the other man / And now we demands a chance / To do things for ourselves." Dad was determined to live the dream, not just sing about it. "I don't want nobody to give me nothing / Open up the door, I'll get it myself," he wrote in another song. And that's what he did. He worked hard and he made it and, by darned, he was going to enjoy the fruits of his labor. If he was the only black man in the neighborhood, well, so be it. He deserved to be there. And if he could do it, others could, too. I can only imagine how it felt for my father, a poor kid from the Terry who grew up in a roadhouse and was once sent home from grammar school for "insufficient clothes," to drive his brand-new Lincoln up to the biggest, baddest house on Walton Way.

It was only as an adult that I began thinking about how much thought Dad put into our Christmas display in Augusta. It said so much about his character. That first year we lived there, he checked out everyone else's decorations, and he must have thought to himself, *What can I do to make sure we're part of the neighborhood?* And like the neighbors, he went all out, ordering custom-made decorations and then hiring a crew to make sure everything was perfectly placed and trimmed. Mr. Brown wanted to fit in—but on his own terms. I'm sure that first year, when he envisioned our Christmas display he was thinking, *I'm going to do this for my family, for my kids, so that they can see I'm as much a part of this community as anyone else.*

But, dang it, I'm going to do it my way.

4

An Ordinary Life

*"The happiest moments of my life have been the few
which I have passed at home in the bosom of my family."*
—Thomas Jefferson

SOMETIMES NOW I think back with wonder at how ordinary our life seemed. Yeah, we always had an inground pool and cool cars. And when I was three and we moved from Walton Way across the Savannah River to Beech Island, South Carolina, we had sixty acres and horses and go-carts and a playhouse Dad made that was a replica of the big house. We brought our black and white pony, Sugar, with us to Beech Island, and, after we settled in, Dad bought two more horses—a sweet white mare we called Mama and a black stallion Dad named Jet. Jet was Dad's horse, and he was more for show than anything else. He was as wild as he was colossal. Dad would dress in his jeans and his cowboy boots and hat and spend hours up at the stables brushing the horses. Sometimes, he walked alongside Deanna and me when we rode Sugar on the trails nearby. But he never saddled Jet. Mom said it was enough for him just to admire the gleaming black stallion; he didn't need to ride him. Dad loved dogs, too, especially boxers, and we had a bunch of them. They lived in the kennels up by the horse barns, and I used to crawl in their cages and take naps with them. Only Mom's dog, an Afghan hound named Fuzzy, was allowed in our house, which I didn't think was fair. Fuzzy's long, silky coat swept the ground, and I remember thinking that he must be hot as the devil with all that hair. I decided to fix that, so one day I snuck a pair of scissors out of Mom's sewing box and convinced my sister that we needed to give Fuzzy a trim. My mom was fit to be tied when she saw her prize dog's precious coat chopped to pieces.

Our Beech Island house was big, but it was nothing spectacular, certainly not by today's standards. You'd never find Diddy or Jay-Z living in a place like that. As successful as Dad was, he was practical and sometimes even stingy, like a lot of people who grew up around the Great Depression. I think Elvis was probably that way, too. I was in my twenties when I saw Graceland for the first time, and I remember how surprised I was that it was so "normal." Our house was a ranch-style, long and L-shaped. There were sliding glass doors leading outside from every room because the previous owners had a fire once; when they rebuilt they wanted to make sure they could never be trapped inside. It had four bedrooms, a baby grand piano in the living room, and sweeping views of the Savannah River, but it was by no means grand. I preferred the house on Walton Way because I liked being able to look out the window and see people and cars, but Mom loved the solitude of Beech Island. Sometimes she'd go outside wearing only her bathing suit.

Life was simple there. My sister and I didn't want for much, but we certainly weren't spoiled, not in the way of the celebrity kids I read about today, such as Suri Cruise, with her Ferragamo purse and $100,000 playhouse. That wasn't us. Oh, we enjoyed the perks of Dad's career, the horses and the nice cars and the special attention that came with his celebrity. But the Brown girls didn't get toys from FAO Schwarz or have designer dresses delivered from the expensive department stores in the city.

Our backyard swing was a piece of plywood between two pieces of rope that dangled from a tree branch, and I swung on it for hours on end. I would pump my legs really hard, swinging as high as they would take me, and imagine my feet touching the clouds. I rarely had trouble entertaining myself, and it's a good thing. When you live behind locked wrought iron gates in a house that can't even be seen from the road, it's not like you can make friends with the neighborhood kids. Besides, Dad didn't trust many people, and he didn't want us fraternizing with anyone but people from his inner circle.

My playmate was my sister. We were best friends. On most days, Deanna and I played hopscotch on the driveway on a hopscotch board we scratched out with pieces of broken bottles we found on the property. Another favorite pastime was making mud pies. We'd pour sand buckets full of water into the red clay in our backyard and then dig in for handfuls of mud and form little pies, which we served with imaginary tea.

Of course, there were lonely days up there on the hill, days when Deanna and I were desperate for companionship other than each other. Sometimes, we'd amble down our long, winding driveway to the guardhouse and peer out of the locked gates, our faces forlorn with boredom, watching for the occasional car to pass. Poor us. We were little prisoners on a sprawling southern estate. On those days, I could hardly wait for the girl from the local YMCA to get there to give me swimming lessons in our pool.

From time to time we had other kids over, but they were always the kids of someone who worked for my Dad. I guess I'd call them "forced friends." Our housekeeper, Miss Ella, used to bring her son to work, and I liked to play with him. Sometimes Dad's band members brought their kids for birthday or pool parties. I always wondered if those kids liked playing with me or if their parents made them because Dad was their meal ticket. *Now be nice to little Yamma if you want all those expensive Christmas gifts this year.*

Dad was on the road more than he was home, so it was usually just Mom, Deanna, Miss Ella, and me. Although my time with him was scarce, the memories I have are as vivid as the spring blooms on a Georgia magnolia tree.

One of my best childhood memories is of wandering away from home one day and sauntering toward the distant field where our horses grazed, hoping I wouldn't get caught before I got there. I was around four at the time, just a wee little girl. Mom and Dad were sleeping late that day, the way they usually did when Dad got home late from a trip. Miss Ella was busy cooking breakfast—I can still smell the aroma of that smoked bacon—when I ducked into the kitchen for a carrot and a handful of sugar cubes.

"Don't wake your Daddy now, Yamma," Miss Ella said, glancing over her shoulder, as bacon sizzled and popped in the cast-iron frying pan on the stove. "He's been working hard and he needs his sleep."

Dad had been away for two weeks, and I knew it would be a day or two before he was rested enough to play with my sister and me. I held my hand with the sugar cubes and the carrot behind my back and headed for the back door.

"I won't," I promised Miss Ella, slipping on my favorite white huarache sandals.

It was late morning when I left, and the air was already thick with the southern summer heat—the soggy, stifling kind of heat that makes it hard to breathe. I was dressed in my favorite yellow cotton sundress, with thin straps and a ruffle around the hem.

Mom had bought it from the Spiegel catalog that spring. I loved it so much I would have worn it every day if she'd have let me. My skin was damp, and strands of hair, loosened from my long braid, stuck to the nape of my neck. I have my father's unruly hair, and the only way to tame it was to pull it back. Still, I always fidgeted as Miss Ella patiently wove the wiry strands into a tight braid after my bath each night. When I woke up, of course, my hair was matted and tangled and looked more like tumbleweed. I was a little kid, though. What did I care?

With Miss Ella's back still to me, I buckled my sandals and walked out of the house and into our garage, then over the hopscotch board that Deanna and I had etched on the driveway. Continuing on, I passed our playhouse in our backyard and, for just a moment, sat on the swing, kicking up red dust with my shoes.

It wasn't unusual for me to be alone outside the house for long periods of time. Miss Ella would stick her head out the door every so often to check on me. Sometimes she came outside and pushed me on the swing or sat on a stool outside the playhouse while I served up the mud cakes and imaginary tea in tiny, pink teacups. After a few minutes, she'd return to her chores inside and I'd continue playing.

I knew I had some time before Miss Ella missed me.

Mom called Miss Ella "her heart." They became acquainted during our customary trips to the S&S Cafeteria for fried chicken and sweet potato balls, after seeing Dad off at the airport in Augusta. Miss Ella had dark brown skin and a smile as white as the bark on a birch tree. She was our favorite waitress at the S&S, and we asked for her every time we went. Tall and stout, she could hoist a heavy tray full of dishes up onto her broad shoulders with a single, swift movement. When she walked, her blue-checkered apron swayed in time with the sound of her rubber-soled shoes squeaking across the floor. Mom said she liked it that Miss Ella was well kept. I liked that she always called me sweetie.

Miss Ella was younger than my mother, but, to me, she looked like a grandmother should. She had an ample waist and gray streaks in her hair, and there was a soft quality about her. One day, after we finished up our dessert of egg custard pie, Mom asked Miss Ella if she wanted to leave her job at the restaurant and come to work as our nanny. Miss Ella's eyes flew open and she said she didn't even have to think about her answer. "Thanks be!" she cried. "When do I start?" I was so happy I shrieked and clapped. Miss Ella clapped, too, and mashed my cheeks between her doughy fingers.

Miss Ella did everything for us. She cooked our meals and washed our clothes and scrubbed our floors 'til they gleamed. Sometimes, she even washed Dad's hair and rolled it in curlers. She became my mother's closest confidante, and she treated me like I was her own child. Mom said she couldn't get through a day if it weren't for Miss Ella. When my father did something to make my mother cry, Miss Ella would hold her in her arms, saying, "Now, now, Miss Brown. Stop your crying. Ain't no use fretting about a man when God loves you." Sometimes I thought I loved Miss Ella more than I did my mom. I knew I shouldn't. But she made me feel cared for and safe.

I also knew I shouldn't be going to see the horses by myself, but sometimes I did things I wasn't supposed to do. As Henry Wadsworth Longfellow wrote, "There was a little girl,/who had a little curl,/right in the middle of her forehead;/When she was good,/she was very good indeed,/But when she was bad she was horrid." I'm pretty sure there were moments when my parents could relate to that little ditty. Like the time, earlier that summer, when Deanna found a cigarette and some matches left over from a visit from one of Dad's business partners and decided to try smoking. Mom was out and Miss Ella was busy somewhere in the house. I followed

Deanna into her room and watched as she lit the cigarette and took a puff, then another. Deanna said she didn't like smoking much. But before she threw the cigarette in the toilet, she handed it to me. The end was wet where Deanna had sucked on it, and bits of bitter-tasting tobacco came off on my tongue. I spit them out, and then took a puff. "Ick!" I cried. Deanna shushed me and then tossed the cigarette in the toilet bowl and flushed. We both watched as it whirled around and around and finally disappeared. Mom came home and smelled the smoke and we both got spankings.

Now, I was about to embark on a journey that was sure to get me a worse licking than that.

Dad sometimes took me in his go-cart to watch the horses graze, so I knew the direction of the pasture. I stopped to look at the asters and blue lilies growing in mom's greenhouse, and then I headed down the grassy hill behind our house and ambled past the pond where Dad fished for sunnies. It looked more like a lake to me. With the pond behind me, I waded through a field of tall Indian grass and goldenrod until I came to the narrow path that led through a patch of pines and up to our dog kennels. I turned to look back and realized I could no longer see our house.

Undeterred, I turned onto the path. The woods were cool and I was happy for the brief respite from the bright sun. As fearless as I was, I always watched out for snakes. One time, Dad and I practically tripped over a big, black snake in the horse stables. It was curled up in a corner of one of the stalls, and it hissed and coiled when it saw us. I wailed and grabbed Daddy's leg and didn't let go. He scooped me up and sat me on a fence rail outside, grabbed a shovel from the barn, and stabbed at the snake, finally cutting its head off. The snake's body kept twisting and squirming, and Dad hit it again and again until it went still. Tossing the shovel aside, he dusted off his cowboy boots and retrieved me. "Yamma," he said, his gravelly voice deadly serious. "You always look out for snakes, you hear? And if you see one and I'm not with you, get away as fast as your little legs will take you." I promised Dad I would.

As I walked out of the woods, back into the sunlight, I spotted the dog kennels up ahead. By then, the sugar cubes were melting in my hand. I popped what was left of them into my mouth, wiped my sticky palm on the skirt of my yellow sundress, and licked my fingers clean.

The dogs went berserk when they saw me, barking and leaping over each other with excitement. I figured they felt the way I did when company came. Ducking under a split rail fence, I walked toward the kennels. I chose the cleanest one and climbed inside with the boxer Dad named Gruff. His cold, wet nose felt good against my warm cheek, and he licked the last remnants of sugar from my hand.

I rested for a while and then moved on, content and unafraid, having not seen any snakes. I picked wildflowers along the way, enough for two small bunches—one for Mom and one for Miss Ella. I don't know how long I was walking when I finally saw the horse pasture up ahead, but it seemed like a long time. I was getting hungry and tired, and my bare legs were bruised and scraped from blackberry brambles and bull thistle. But any discomfort I felt disappeared when I saw my pony.

"Sugar!" I cried, running toward the fenced meadow. "Sugar, it's me! It's Yamma!"

I could tell Sugar was happy to see me. She nickered and loped over to the split rail fence where I stood, sweaty and dirty, still clutching the carrot in my hand. I could see Jet and Mama grazing off in the distance. I was glad they were far away, because I was kind of scared of Jet.

I put my foot on the bottom rail of the fence and reached for the top one with both hands, trying to pull myself up, to get nearer to Sugar. I slipped off the rail, scraping my arm, and tried again. But I barely had time to lift myself up when I heard my father's raspy voice echoing in the distance.

"Yamma!" he cried. "Yamma! Where are you, baby? Yamma!"

I had never heard my Dad sound so frightened. It scared me and I began to whimper. "I'm here, Daddy. Over here, with Sugar," I cried.

My father couldn't hear me. He was still too far away and my voice was too small to carry. He kept calling me, getting louder and louder each time.

"Yamma! Come to Daddy, baby. Yamma! Yaaaaaa-mmmmmaaaaaaaa!"

I saw him before he saw me. He was running frantically through an adjacent field, headed I don't know where. His chest was bare and he had on the black sweatpants he always pulled on when he got out of bed in the morning.

"Daddy!" I called, waving my hands in the air. "Daddy! I'm over here! Over here with Sugar!"

The moment my father spotted me, he stopped running and his whole body collapsed into itself. He fell to his knees, dropping his head into his hands. A few seconds passed, and then he picked himself up off the ground and began to run toward me. As he came closer, I could see the sweat rolling off his face and down his bare chest. His pants were covered with thorns, and his hair was sticking out every which way. His leather house slippers were caked with red clay dust.

I always knew my father loved me. He was serious and reserved at home, but he never turned away from a hug from either of his girls. And when we misbehaved, Mom always did the spanking because Dad couldn't bear to lay a hand on us. Mom always said I was Daddy's little girl, but I never felt that more than when I saw the tears rolling down his cheeks when he finally found me that day up in the horse meadow. He practically tackled me, scooping me up in his muscular arms. I could feel the heavy pounding of his heart as he held me tight to his heaving chest. Between my own tears and his fierce embrace, I could hardly breathe.

"I'm sorry, Daddy," I managed to say.

Dad looked down into my eyes. He shook his head. "Yamma, my little Yammacakes!" he cried, over and over, his raw voice choked with relief.

He rocked me for a few minutes and then finally loosened his grip and set me down on the grass. He wiped the dirt from my cheeks and looked me up and down, from my soiled dress to my scratched legs and grass-stained sandals.

"Yamma," he cried, his voice squeaking. "Dang it! Where in the world have you been?"

The meadow was quiet except for the sound of Sugar whinnying and her hooves crunching on the dry grass.

"C'mon now," Dad said. "Your mama and Miss Ella are worried sick. Everyone's out looking for you."

We had only taken a few steps when I realized that I still had the carrot in my hand. I stopped walking.

"Wait, Daddy! Wait!" I cried, running back to my pony.

I tossed the carrot over the fence to Sugar and waited while she chewed it with her long, brown teeth. Then I ran back to my dad. He took my hand and we headed home.

Some of my best memories are from the house in Beech Island. As a child, whenever I was sad or afraid, I was able to close my eyes and revive the warm moments with Dad.

It was how I was able to drown out the smacking sound of his fists when he was beating the crap out of Mom.

5

Dad's Beating Mom Again

"Be very careful if you make a woman cry, because God
counts her tears. The woman came out of a man's rib. Not from
his feet to be walked on. Not from his head to be superior,
but from the side to be equal. Under the arm to be protected,
and next to the heart to be loved."
—*English translation from the Talmud by A. W. Streane*

THE BEATINGS ALWAYS began the same way, with the same terrible sounds. My parents are in their bedroom, behind closed doors. First comes the boom of my father's voice. "Dee Dee! Goddamn it, Dee Dee!" Then I hear what sounds like thunder rolling through the house. That's mom hitting the wall. I wait for her to scream, but she doesn't. She whimpers. She must have learned long ago that screaming incites him. I'm scared shitless, of course. If he can do this to her, what if one of these times he goes ape shit on me? Who's going to protect me? Certainly not her. She doesn't even try to defend herself, and I kind of hate her for that. I don't know of any other kids whose fathers beat their mothers. But I don't know that many kids, so who knows? If he should decide to attack me, Deanna can't help. She's older than me but just as scared. What if he kills Mom?

Even as a little kid I knew that men weren't supposed to hit women. I'm not sure how I knew; I think maybe Deanna told me. But how would she know? We had lived with this crap since we were sucking on bottles. I kept thinking that one of these times Mom was going to die.

I swear that during those fights, and they happened a lot, I could feel the whole house shake with my father's crazy rage. Whenever he'd start, Deanna and I would run for cover, usually in a closet or under our beds, and cry quietly into our cupped hands. I shook a lot as a kid. My hands. My face. My knees. A five-year-old with tremors. As my grandma used to say, "Ain't that just the saddest thing?" Sometimes the fights lasted only minutes. Sometimes longer. The monster would appear, wreaking havoc on our lives, and then the rumbling would stop and we'd hear our mother's muffled cries. After that, the house would go completely quiet. The sound of the silence was the worst, believe it or not. Because that's when Deanna and I would huddle up in a ball, waiting for our mother to surface, wondering if she were alive or dead and if we would be next.

My father never beat us, but he might as well have. Sometimes I think a beating would have been less hurtful than hearing the sounds of him using my mother as his punching bag. Sometimes I threw up in my hands when they fought. Usually I just shook like a damn leaf trying to hold on during a brisk fall breeze. When my father was in that crazy-ass way, everything was my mother's fault. She couldn't do anything right. When he started, she took it to the bedroom and closed the doors—I presume to spare Deanna and me from seeing her battered. Every time it happened, I was terrified for my mother and was sure I must have done something to contribute to my father's rages, yet I was helpless to do anything to stop the fights.

I wasn't even in kindergarten the first time I realized that the sounds coming from my parents' room meant danger. I'd hear bumping sounds, like furniture being moved, and Mom crying, "Stop, James! James! Stop!" I don't recall ever hearing my father's voice, but from what I did hear, I could only imagine what was going on inside that room. It became clear when mom emerged, crying, with red welts on her face and body.

As much as I loved my father, and I sure loved him, I hated him during those times. And I didn't like my mother much either. Even as a little girl, I didn't understand why she let my father treat her like that. I resented that she was always walking on eggshells, trying not to start anything, and it didn't take much to get something going. If she couldn't stand up for herself, how would she protect me? What if I slipped up and did or said something Dad didn't like and he decided to turn on me, his little Yammacakes? I didn't *think* he'd hurt me, but I couldn't be sure. I couldn't possibly defend myself against a strong man like my father, especially not when he was in one of his rages. One punch and I was a goner, no doubt about it. I was pretty sure my mother wouldn't step in to help me. She would probably act as if it wasn't happening, which is what she did after every time Dad thrashed her: pretend it hadn't happened.

"What's wrong, Mommy?"

"Nothing's wrong, Yamma."

"But your lip's bleeding, Mommy."

"I said I'm fine."

"Why was Daddy yelling at you?"

"What are you talking about?"

"Why are you crying, Mommy?"

"I'm not crying."

Confused kid? Gee, I wonder why. Sometimes when I said my prayers before bed, I'd ask God for peace. *Now I lay me down to sleep, I pray the Lord that Dad doesn't start.* Sometimes my prayers were answered, usually when Dad was on the road and it was just Mom, Deanna, and me. Other times my prayers seemed to go unheard, no matter how hard I talked to God, trying to drown out the sounds of my father's angry voice and my mother's cries. After a while, I did what my mom did and acted as if the beatings hadn't happened. I'd pretend the Browns were just like everyone else, a happily married couple with their two great kids.

But it was hard to pretend after I witnessed one of those brutal beatings, the first and only time I actually saw, and not just heard, the brutality that my father was capable of.

It was a sultry summer day, and Deanna and I were happy to be playing a game in our air-conditioned house when the screams and the banging began. We knew the drill and quickly climbed under the coffee table in the living room and held our ears, waiting for the sounds to stop. But this time was different. Waiting for the silence, I heard the bedroom door slam and the sounds of footsteps rumbling down the hallway. *Boom boom boom boom boom!* The footsteps got louder and closer. Louder and closer. Deanna and I squeezed each other tightly, holding on for dear life. From our hiding spot under the coffee table we could see my mother pad past the living room in her bare feet, with my father on the edge of her heels. The clack of his boots hitting the tile floor made me shake and cringe. I could hear his heavy, rasping breaths. This wasn't my father. This was the enemy, a madman stalking his prey.

Cowering under the table, I watched as the two pairs of feet moved toward the front door. My mother was crying. I saw my father lunge forward to grab her, and she leaped forward and screamed. *"James! Stop! James! Please! Ahhhhhhh!"* I had never heard her sound so afraid. The front door flew open, and they were outside. "Daddy's going to kill her," I said to my sister. "We have to do something."

I was five years old.

I ran to the front door and peered outside. I can still see vividly what I saw that day. My mother was dressed in her blue and white robe. Her legs were splayed wide open and my father was straddling her, pummeling her with clenched fists. *Doosh. Thud. Doosh. Thud.* Blood spurted from my mother's face. She started thrashing around, kicking her legs, holding up her arms to ward off the punches and trying to break free, trying to save herself. I froze in place, but then something inside of me took over and I knew I had to do something. I felt no fear, only rage. I ran outside, screaming, "Leave her alone! Stop punching Mommy!" He didn't even turn around. He just kept punching. The next thing I knew I was on his back, trying to pull him off of my mom. Sweat was dripping off his face and his eyes were glazed and wild. When he first looked at me, it was as if I was looking into the eyes of a stranger—and a mad one at that. "Stop!" I screamed. "Leave Mommy alone!" My father looked stunned. It was as if he'd awakened from a bad dream. His head dropped and his shoulders slumped. I looked down at my mom. Her eyes were purple and her face was bloody. She didn't look back at me.

Years later, when I asked my mom about the beatings and reminded her about the only one I ever actually saw, she said it was that very day she made up her mind to leave my father. That day, something inside her said that if she didn't leave, someone was going to end up dead, and she was pretty sure it would be her. But by the time she made her decision, the damage had already been done to me. I'd been programmed to accept abuse as part of life.

Years later I read a quote by Stephen King that summed up what it was like, living with the abuse: "People outside such relationships will sometimes ask, 'How could you let such a business go on for so many years? Didn't you see the elephant in the living room?' And it's so hard for anyone living in a more normal situation to understand the answer that comes closest to the truth; 'I'm sorry, but it was there when I moved in. I didn't know it was an elephant; I thought it was part of the furniture.'"

I was in college before I stopped trembling every time my father raised his voice. He could be shouting at a business associate over the phone and I'd be quaking in a corner somewhere. I didn't need a psychiatrist to tell me that witnessing my father beating on my mother like she was a Mexican piñata would have a profound effect on me.

It probably would have helped if someone had warned me that children who live with abuse often become abusers or victims themselves. But no one warned me about that. So, by the time I was old enough to date, I promised myself that no man would ever treat me the way I saw my father treat my mom. God help the man who took a hand to me. I wouldn't stand for it. Never.

But when it did happen, I didn't know it was an elephant. I thought it was part of the furniture.

6

Leaving Dad

"God sometimes removes a person from your life for your protection. Don't run after them."

—Pastor Rick Warren

I GET MAD every time I read the part of my father's autobiography that talks about the end of my parents' marriage. He wrote in his book that the reason for the breakup was that Mom couldn't handle being married to an entertainer. She wanted someone who was home every night. "She might say there was some other reason that we broke up," Dad wrote in *James Brown: The Godfather of Soul*, "but I believe that my being an entertainer was the reason." Maybe that's what my father needed to believe, but I'm afraid he had a selective memory. My parents' marriage ended because he was violent and she was tired of being beat up and put down. My mother was sick of being afraid of her own husband, of somehow innocently provoking his rage. *If I do this, will it set him off? If I don't do that, will he snap?* Imagine living that way, never knowing what will trigger your abuser, being afraid to make the simplest move or decision for fear you could be punished, even killed, by someone who is supposed to love you.

I'm sorry Dad never owned up to the abuse, at least not in writing. In his book, he remembers the actual breakup this way:

> I was working somewhere—I don't even remember where—and I left early to be with my family on Valentine's Day. I wanted to have a candlelight dinner and then a long talk about us to see if we could work it out. When I came up the drive she already had the station wagon packed and the two girls inside ready to leave. I talked to her. I argued with her, but it didn't do any good. She left and took the girls with her. I watched them go down the drive until they were out of sight at the bottom of the hill, heading toward the front gate. I stood there in the middle of all that land, by myself, just listening to that car fade away.

It's a sad story, but it's total fiction.

I was seven years old when we drove away from Beech Island with little more than the clothes from our closets. The memory of that night is grainy, like the pictures in our old family albums, and the significance of what was happening only became clear many weeks later when I realized we weren't going home. But I recently asked my mother and sister for their recollections of that time, and their versions matched mine.

It was toward the end of October, around Halloween, not on Valentine's Day as my father recalled. And he was on the road at the time, not at home in South Carolina. Deanna and I were at a costume party at a friend's house, and Mom picked us up with her station wagon so loaded with stuff there was barely room to sit. "Where are we going?" I asked, squeezing into a small space in the back of the car. "We're going to Ninnie's," my mother answered, without elaboration. Ninnie was my mom's mother, and we saw her rarely, only for short visits. I figured this was one of those times.

Mom drove most of the night, first stopping in Virginia to visit relatives on her father's side, then on to Ninnie's in Washington, DC. For me it was an adventure. We were on a road trip. I loved riding in the car. It never occurred to me that we were leaving my dad. Not until one night when I heard Mom telling Ninnie that we wouldn't be going back. Things at home were bad, Mom told Ninnie. She had tried her best to keep the marriage together, she said, and she still loved James, but sometimes he turned into a monster and during those times she feared for her life and our safety. My stomach went all fluttery as I listened to what my mother was saying. She sounded sad but resolute. Even then, I didn't believe our new arrangement was something permanent. *It would be OK,* I told myself. *They're just mad at each other. Maybe she needs some time.*

Three weeks passed, then four. No one said anything, but I finally realized we really weren't going home and I started to get scared. The family as I knew it was gone. My feelings were jumbled and confused. I knew Daddy wasn't a nice person sometimes, especially to my mother—and it would be years before I discovered that his demon was drugs—but I didn't want to leave him. I worried that he'd be lonesome without his girls. At the same time, I was glad my mom would finally have some peace. And I didn't have to be afraid anymore.

We stayed at my grandmother's place until Mom was able to get on her feet. As soon as she had a job, we moved to the fledgling Maryland suburb of Crofton, into a rented townhouse in a nice middle-class development with lots of kids. Crofton is exactly halfway between Washington and Baltimore, where my mother grew up, about twenty miles from each city, and it has the distinction of twice being named one of *Money* magazine's "100 Best Places to

Live." When we arrived there in the late 1970s it was only a little more than fifteen years old but already well settled, with a community golf club, a town green, and subdivisions sprouting up all over the landscape. I've read that the founders of the town chose its name based on the criteria that it sounded like a pleasant place to live, and it was.

I guess I finally realized Crofton was home when Mom enrolled us in school there. Deanna and I had gone to a private Christian school when we were living in Beech Island. There wasn't money for expensive private schools anymore, so public school it was. Our busy little suburb was so different than the tranquility of the southern woods. We had moved from a virtual island of privacy to a town with lots of people and cars and things to do. And we were virtually anonymous.

Mom took a job at the telephone company, and she wasn't around as much as I would have liked. She always seemed to be working. Miss Ella stayed on with Dad and we didn't have a housekeeper anymore, so my sister and I helped with the household chores, cleaning our rooms, vacuuming and dusting, doing dishes, stuff like that. When Mom was late getting home from work, I'd help my sister start dinner. Eventually my grandparents moved in with us to help out. My mother needed to work long hours to be able to meet the bills, believe it or not, and even at my tender age I knew it wasn't right that Dad was rich and famous and we were struggling to pay the electric bill. I had watched my mom take my father's abuse for so long, and then she leaves and has to fight to keep a roof over our heads? There was nothing fair about it. My father wouldn't help her out. Not only that, he fought *not* to have to help support us, his children. I won't embarrass my mother or disrespect my father by telling you how much he ended up having to pay in child support, but he could have done—and should have done—much better. Still, what we lost in lifestyle when we left my dad, we gained in normalcy. My mother wasn't watching everything she said and did, and she was no longer aloof and withdrawn. She wanted to do whatever she could to make sure Deanna and I were OK. And she was getting her own life back. She was starting over, just like we were. In a way, we were all just getting to really know each other.

Looking back, I realize how strange it was that my mother didn't tell us we were leaving my father. I'm a mother and I try to always be honest with my kids. I think she was probably afraid, because Dad was the center of our universe. James Brown's celebrity didn't end when he stepped offstage. When my father was home, he insisted on having our undivided attention, and we were happy to oblige. We couldn't even listen to records by other artists without Dad getting mad. I remember one time he blew up at us when he came home from a road tour and we were playing our favorite Natalie Cole record—repeatedly and loudly. He burst into our room, all bent out of shape and demanded to know, "Why are you listening to *her*? Why aren't you listening to James Brown?" That was the end of Natalie.

My father was everything to us. Mom had always been there, but early memories of her are scarce because Dad was her focus and we spent more time with Miss Ella than we did with her. Miss Ella fed us and dressed us and made sure we got where we were supposed to go. She also played the role of my mother's confidante, her shoulder to cry on. My father was thirteen years older than my mother. She was still in high school when she met him in 1966 while he was performing in Baltimore. They married four years later on the front porch of a probate judge in Dad's hometown of Barnwell, South Carolina. For the fifteen years they were together, my mother was at his beck and call. Being the wife of James Brown was all she knew how to be. Now she was in her early thirties and free as a bird. I have to say that independence suited her.

Deanna and I discovered our own kind of freedom in Crofton. For the first time we were allowed to make our own acquaintances. Dad had always been so overly protective that we weren't allowed to have friends in Beech Island, not unless they were the kids of his friends, and it got mighty lonely sometimes. Now we were riding bicycles and playing hopscotch in the street after school with the neighborhood kids. We didn't have much in the way of riches or special attention, but we had a kind of normalcy I had never known before. For the first time in my life, I was just another kid. I was anonymous, and I was carefree.

And I liked it.

7

A New Life

*"It was a splendid summer morning and it seemed as if
nothing could go wrong."*

—John Cheever, "The Common Day"

MY PARENTS' DIVORCE was final in January 1981. Dad hadn't come around much after the separation, but now we would see him more than ever before. Part of the divorce settlement was a stipulation that Deanna and I would spend summers with Dad. I was nine years old and living two separate lives. At home, I was a shy kid living a barely middle-class life. A lot of the kids didn't even know who my father was. I made my bed in the morning and washed the dinner dishes at night. When I stayed with Dad, I lived like a princess, flying places in private jets and riding around in limousines, staying in the best hotels and hobnobbing with celebrities. Wherever we went, people rolled out the red carpet. Dad took us to amusement parks and we were escorted to the front of the line for every ride. Can you imagine the scene? We're walking through Six Flags. First, you notice the hair, and then you recognize the voice. Then, James Brown himself hops on the ride next to you. I loved watching people's reactions when they recognized him. We walked into crowded restaurants and were seated before everyone else. Everywhere we went it was "Yes, Mr. Brown." "Of course, Mr. Brown." "Whatever you'd like, Mr. Brown." It was those times that it was cool to have a famous father. But my best memories are of those simple times when my father wasn't playing the role of James Brown but when he was just being my dad. Those family outings were among the rare times that he let his guard down. He seemed to enjoy every moment, and we did, too.

My father wasn't openly affectionate, but I knew he loved us. When it was just him and his girls, he seemed happy, and he was fun to be around. We'd often take long drives along bumpy country roads in his black van, passing corn and soybean fields and groves of tall pines along the way. Beech Island was pretty rural then, and you usually had to drive a ways to get somewhere. My father's favorite foot-long chili dogs were several towns away, but that never stopped us from hopping in the van and going. "How about a chili dog, Yammacakes?" he'd ask in that raspy voice. He'd order, then chomp down his dog with his gleaming white teeth, and he was in heaven. I pretended to love them, too, just to make him happy, but I could barely get one down.

Dad loved to drive, and he drove himself around a lot. It all seemed so wonderfully normal to be in the car, riding around anonymously, until he'd stop to pump his own gas. Of course he was always recognized. He'd be standing outside the van, and people screamed and clamored for his attention. He'd sign autographs and speak to everyone. Especially kids. He never turned a child away. Deanna and I would be pouting in the back of the van. *Would he just hurry up already?*

Those were the days when everything seemed so easy. The best times were summer mornings, and they always started the same way. Dad usually slept late after staying up watching old westerns on TV. He'd amble downstairs in his robe and fix the same breakfast, Cornflakes and milk with bananas sliced on top. When he was finished with his cereal, he'd place his empty bowl on the kitchen counter, Miss Ella's cue that it was time to style his hair. (He always said hair and teeth made the man, and both his hair and his teeth gleamed.) Miss Ella would drag in this big bag of curlers, yellow and pink, with picks and combs and bottles of styling sprays and gels, B&B and Wella Balsam and Finisheen. For the next half hour or so, Miss Ella would carefully separate his shiny black hair into sections with a pick, comb in setting gel, and roll each section with the huge foam curlers. After his hair was set, she'd cover his head with a black hairnet. Then Dad was ready for his audience.

Sometimes, he'd stay in the kitchen or move to the adjoining den or the pool house and take a seat under one of his bubble salon-style hairdryers. Deanna and I sat at his knee, and as the hairdryer blasted out heat, he regaled us with his favorite stories. We were a captive audience, but there was no place I would have rather been than sitting with my father, listening to him talk about growing up in the Terry or marching for civil rights or dining with presidents in the White House. (Over the course of his lifetime, my father visited the White House numerous times, during the terms of Lyndon Johnson, Richard Nixon, Jimmy Carter, George H. W. Bush, Bill Clinton, and George W. Bush.) He could have been talking about thread counts or the price of corn. I didn't care. Because for the time he was under the dryer, he was all mine.

My father presented himself in public as a humble man, but in reality he was egocentric. All of his stories were about him. He used to tell us what a great entertainer he was and how much he had done for the music industry. He'd talk about a concert he'd given in Las Vegas or London and how he'd packed 'em in until there wasn't an empty seat in the house. "You'll never know how big I am until I'm not here anymore." It was as if he were trying to tell us, "You're part of this history, too." Every one of his yarns began the same way. "Did I tell you the story about . . . ?" My favorite stories were from his childhood. Shining shoes in the Terry for the soldiers passing through. Singing in church before he learned to walk. Mastering "Oh, Susannah" on the harmonica by the time he was five. Being born dead in his parents' one-room shack in the pinewoods with his father and two aunts attending the birth. Had it not been for the persistence of Aunt Minnie, there wouldn't be a James Brown, music legend, Dad would say. When everyone else had given up trying to get Baby James to take his first breath, Aunt Minnie shook him and blew into his mouth until he finally took his first scream. Dad loved telling that story. Another he told too many times to count was how, at seven years old, he began performing for the soldiers from nearby Fort Gordon who passed through the Terry. He'd tell us how he'd wait on the canal bridge for the truck convoys and then buck dance as soldiers tossed nickels and dimes and, on really good days, quarters his way. I think that was my all-time favorite. When he told that story, I closed my eyes and imagined him dancing—*Shuffle. Kick. Stamp. Shuffle. Kick. Stamp.*— then collecting all that change, stuffing it into the pockets of his burlap pants and running home to show Aunt Honey the fruits of his labor.

I learned more about my father from those summer storytelling sessions than I ever did from living with him full-time. He told us about coming up in the music business, about performing for the troops in Vietnam and playing to a full Yankee Stadium. I especially loved the tales of his encounters with his fellow superstars. Elvis. Mick Jagger. The Jackson Five. One of my all-time favorites is the one where he took a call from a beleaguered Bill Clinton during the Monica Lewinsky scandal and told the president of the United States, "Yes, what you did was wrong, but we're going to get through this." I laugh when I think about it—my father playing the role of father confessor to the president of the United States.

As much as I loved those moments with my father, I was always anxious to get back home to Crofton, even though there a restaurant meal was reserved for special occasions and our mode of transportation was Mom's used Toyota Camry. When we tried to smuggle even a little bit of elitist behavior back into our average life, Mom gave us that look that said, "Don't even try to bring that attitude into our home."

I had two of those magical summers with Dad before he met a woman named Adrienne Rodriguez and life turned crazy again.

8

Adrienne

*"We know so little about one another. We embrace a shadow
and love a dream."*

—Hjalmar Söderberg, Doctor Glas

TWO YEARS AFTER we left my father, I met his next future wife. Her name was Adrienne Rodriguez, and she had exotically painted eyes under a storm cloud of jet-black hair. To me, an awkward eleven-year-old, she looked like a movie star. Dad met Adrienne on the set of the television show *Solid Gold*, where she was working as a makeup artist. He described in his memoir the first time they saw each other: "We met, our eyes locked, our souls touched. By the end of the taping, without having to say or do anything, we both knew that we were in love." I still can't believe my father wrote that. He just wasn't a mushy kind of guy.

Our introduction took place at my grandfather's funeral (my mother's father) in 1983 in Baltimore. My parents were on speaking terms by then. Even though I'm sure they still loved each other, they knew they couldn't be together and they'd forged a cordial truce. Dad flew in for the service with his new love in tow. He introduced her to my sister and me as "Miss Adrienne." He was proper that way. He insisted we address all adults formally. I liked Adrienne right away. She had an easy smile, and she was respectfully demure. I'm sure she had heard plenty about my mom. She was already living in our former home, and it had my mother's imprint all over it. If she was threatened at all, she didn't show it.

Not that day.

We all tried to make the best of the somber occasion. I had been there alongside my mom when my grandpa had his heart attack. We took turns trying to revive him with CPR. It was a huge loss for us all, my father included. Dad loved my grandfather. They were good friends and remained so even after my parents' divorce. I could see the pain on his face when he walked into the funeral parlor that day. Except for our visits to Beech Island—and we were often left in the care of Miss Ella when we were there because Dad was working—Deanna and I rarely saw our father anymore. So even under those sad circumstances I was thrilled to see him.

I could tell by the way Dad treated Adrienne—with great care, as if she were a fragile china doll—that he was smitten with her, and I wanted her to like me. Their first date had been with Rev. Sharpton, which didn't sound very romantic to me, but Adrienne would later describe those early days of their relationship as blissful. "James was very sincere," she once told an interviewer. "He was a country boy. He said, 'Yes, ma'am; no, ma'am.' He courted me."

A few months after our meeting, a justice of the peace in Beech Island married Dad and Adrienne. It was a small ceremony, with only my grandfather from my father's side in attendance. I learned about it sometime later when Dad called to tell us the news. I was excited for summer to come so I could get to know my new stepmother. Little did I know that nice lady was ushering us into the worst period of my father's life, a decade of madness fueled by drugs and violence.

Let me start by saying that Adrienne and I had a mutual affection for each other right from the start. During our first summer together in Beech Island, I spent most of my time with her while my father went on the road. She couldn't have kids of her own, so whatever maternal instincts she had, she lavished on me. She looked a lot like my mom, and she used to tell me that I could easily be taken for her daughter. Maybe it was the resemblance, or because I was the youngest, but she clearly favored me over my sister. She showed me how to apply lipstick and eye shadow and how to style my hair. And I loved it when she applied long, fake nails to my fingers and painted them bright colors. She loved music, and we often sang together. I can recall us sitting at the piano in the living room singing "Greensleeves." Sometimes she told me stories about her childhood, about how she came from a very poor family and spent most of her youth in foster homes. It felt as if she needed someone to talk to, and I was happy to be the chosen one.

The honeymoon ended with that first summer together. After that, I began to see things that didn't fit into my fantasy of a happy ending. My father and Adrienne had a volatile relationship. One minute they were affectionate with each other, calling each other Sugar, and the next minute they were at each other's throats. There was no such thing as a civil disagreement. They fought dirty and often. Adrienne was wickedly jealous, and that's what usually triggered their fights. It was because of that jealous streak that I learned about my father's lifelong affair with a woman from town named Estelle Johnson.

I was thirteen or fourteen years old, so it was either my second or third summer with Adrienne and Dad. Adrienne and I were headed into Augusta to meet Dad for dinner. Everything was fine until we drove past my father's office. Without a whiff of warning, she slammed on the brakes, turned the car around in the middle of the road, and screeched into the parking lot of his building. Her face was bright red and she was swearing like a truck driver. I didn't know what was happening. The lot was empty except for my father's pickup truck and an older model Lincoln Continental. Dad must have seen us coming (he probably heard the squeal of the tires), because he met us at the front door. Adrienne pushed past him, but the door leading inside was locked. That made her even madder. Her eyes were fiery, and she was ranting like a dang lunatic. As my father watched, bemused, she threw her full weight against the office door and busted it in. The door flew open. All I saw was Miss Johnson's backside, and I'm telling you that woman was scared and scrambling for the back exit. Adrienne followed her outside, picked up a piece of lumber, and chased her across the parking lot. Luckily Miss Johnson was able to get into her car before she was hit over the head with a two-by-four. That dented old Lincoln roared out of the parking lot, narrowly missing oncoming cars in the street. We never made it to the restaurant that night. Adrienne and I went straight home and ate dinner there. When Dad finally arrived, angry words flew back and forth, and he ended up leaving and not returning that night. I found myself in the middle of a marital scuffle I wanted no part of. It wouldn't be the last time that happened.

Adrienne later told me that my father had been seeing Miss Johnson for years, throughout all of his relationships, including his marriage to my mother. (I would later learn that my mother knew about her, too.) My father had assured Adrienne shortly after she came into the picture that Miss Johnson was out of his life for good. She'd always suspected otherwise, so when she saw Miss Johnson's car in the lot, it validated her suspicions and she went berserk. I certainly couldn't blame her. If my father saw Miss Johnson after that day, he must have been much more discreet, because she was still alive when my father died. She came to his funeral.

That same summer I started noticing a side of Adrienne I didn't much like, a side that was moody and mean. She seemed jealous of any attention my father gave Deanna and me, and she didn't want to hear any mention of my mother. When the subject did come up, she would say defiantly, "But I'm James Brown's wife now!" She often seemed to be itching for a confrontation, and it didn't take much for her to get Dad going. She'd usually start by accusing him of still being in love with my mother, and they'd be off. During those times, I hid in my room with my hands over my ears. There were times when the police were called to the house. We had days of great happiness with lots of love and laughter and days of darkness. It seemed to me that, unlike my mother, Adrienne often initiated the fights and she rarely backed off. She could often be short with me, but I hated it even more when she picked on my sister, which she seemed to do relentlessly on her bad days. Sometimes she made up stories about both of us, telling Dad that Deanna and I had been acting up or talking back to her and not treating her with the respect she was due. He'd be mad at us, of course. When we started complaining that her stories were exaggerated and, in some cases, complete fabrications, he dismissed us without ever really hearing us out.

Over time, I learned to tiptoe around Adrienne and Dad. The last thing I wanted was to alienate my father. I wanted so much for him to be part of my life, but I knew if I said something he didn't like or didn't want to deal with, it would jeopardize our relationship. It was that way with everyone who was around my father. No one ever challenged him. He was always right. It was on his terms that you were allowed a piece of him, and he'd cut you off *like that* if you did something he didn't like. Instinctively I knew that if it came down to it, he'd choose Adrienne over Deanna and me. I didn't want to lose him, so I did whatever it took to keep the peace. It was a coping mechanism I carried into adulthood and used in my own abusive marriage.

Adrienne's behavior grew increasingly erratic and Dad finally admitted to me that she abused drugs. He said he didn't like it either when she acted crazy, that he'd tried to get her to stop, but she was hooked. I'd seen her pop pills, but I always assumed they were prescriptions for a medical condition. Apparently the only condition she had back then was a need to get high. That surprised me, but it was nothing compared with what I was about to learn about my father.

Adrienne was always complaining about Dad's smoking. I had seen him light up a time or two, but he didn't seem to have a cigarette habit. I wondered why she couldn't just let it go. It didn't seem like a big deal. Then, one day, when she wasn't getting the attention I guess she thought she deserved, she took me upstairs to their bedroom and showed me what was in some of those cigarettes Dad smoked. My father was in his mid-fifties by then and I had rarely even seen him drink alcohol, so I would have never suspected him of using drugs. Adrienne set me straight about that. My father was abusing street drugs, she said, and she seemed to enjoy telling me that devastating news. She said that, specifically, he used something called PCP—angel dust—a potent white powder that he smoked to get high. Adrienne said the reason *she* took pills was to help her cope when my father was strung out.

I was flabbergasted. Up to that point, I had never witnessed my father drunk or high or, if I did, I didn't recognize it for what it was. Sometimes his behavior was bizarre and over the top, but I chalked it up to the stressors of being an iconic entertainer. Was it possible he had been high way back when he beat my mother? Maybe. Or maybe I needed to believe that because it was an excuse for inexcusable behavior. Looking back, I think that maybe our leaving and his fear of being alone triggered Dad's use of drugs. I'm sure he was thinking, "My wife is gone. My girls are gone. I don't have anybody." All I could think about was how this musical genius had kept his nose clean for most of his life, but in middle age he started using drugs. Just as his music career was resurging? Or was it really like that? I was young and wanted to believe that my father didn't have those problems. The reality was that he had been using drugs for years; I just didn't know it. Now his habit was spiraling out of control. Dad had just had his biggest hit in decades with the song "Living in America" and he'd been inducted as a charter member of the Rock and Roll Hall of Fame. He later told one biographer that on the night he was inducted, "I think I felt for the first time that the struggle was over." If only that had been true.

How could he risk his reputation now? I wondered. *What if he hurts himself? What if he dies?* My first concern was for Dad. Then that self-centered teenage voice intervened, and it was angry. *What if it got out that my father used drugs? What would my friends think? What would the kids back in Crofton say? How could he do this to us? How could he do this to me?* I was about to learn about the downside of having a famous father.

After that, the lessons just kept on coming.

9

Crazy Love

"Usually adult males who are unable to make emotional connections with the women they choose to be intimate with are frozen in time, unable to allow themselves to love for fear that the loved one will abandon them. If the first woman they passionately loved, the mother, was not true to her bond of love, then how can they trust that their partner will be true to love? Often in their adult relationships these men act out again and again to test their partner's love. While the rejected adolescent boy imagines that he can no longer receive his mother's love because he is not worthy, as a grown man he may act out in ways that are unworthy and yet demand of the woman in his life that she offer him unconditional love."
—bell hooks, The Will To Change: Men, Masculinity, and Love

IN SOME WAYS Adrienne did me a favor by telling me my father's secret. At least I wasn't blindsided by the events that were soon to transpire with the inevitability of falling dominoes. Shortly after I got the news, Dad began self-destructing in public. The timing

for me couldn't have been worse. I had just begun attending Arch-
bishop Keough High School, an all-girls Catholic school in Baltimore, and was trying to make new friends. It seemed like every
week there was another embarrassing story in the press.

Every time the police went to the Beech Island house on a
domestic violence call, someone wrote about it. Dad and Adrienne
were airing their problems in public and every media outlet from
New York to California reported on them. There were charges
and countercharges. One minute they were accusing each other of
some crazy behavior—he planted drugs in her purse, she set fire
to his clothes, he shot holes in her sable coat, she planted drugs
in his nasal inhaler—the next minute they were professing their
total devotion to one another. Some of the stories were so absurd
they were laughable. One time, Adrienne was charged with driving
under the influence of drugs, and she tried to beat the rap by claiming "diplomatic immunity" as the wife of the "Ambassador of Soul."
The media had a field day with that.

I was an all-around good student but kind of shy. I loved math
and science and played on the field hockey and lacrosse teams,
but my confidence was as shaky as most other teenage girls. The
antics of Dad and Adrienne brought me attention I didn't want.
As proud as I was to be the daughter of a celebrity, I wanted to
be Yamma Anybody-but-Brown when Dad began making headlines for biting Adrienne in the face or giving her a black eye or
when Adrienne was arrested for trying to smuggle PCP through
the airport or charging my father with some diabolical behavior.
It's tough enough being a teenage girl, what with all the boy drama
and the bouncing hormones and not enough hours in the day to
fit in school and sports and homework and friends. Add to that
equation a very famous father and his wife whose misbehavior was

reported in the back pages of every newspaper in the country, and it's a wonder I did so well in school.

The worst time was in April 1986, shortly after Dad filed for divorce from Adrienne and after a fight that brought police to their house and got Dad arrested. He showed up on CNN high out of his mind. He was wearing colored glasses, yellow, and he was slurring his words and making a fool of himself. The performance earned him the number four slot on the "Twenty Weirdest TV Interviews of All Time" by Nerve.com in 2009. It's hard to imagine there were any weirder TV moments, certainly not from my vantage point. Unfortunately, that four-minute interview has more than six million views on YouTube, more than any of his music performances. Dad was acting foolish, and he was rude to the interviewer. When she questioned him about the latest assault on Adrienne, his eyes popped and he slurred, "Let's talk about some music! I'm concerned, because there's nothing wrong. The charges were dropped out of love. I'm single and I want to mingle!"

The interviewer tried to change the subject to his upcoming tour. "The women love you when you get out there. Why is that?" she asked. "Why? Because I smell good. I make love good!" Dad replied, one word slurring into the next.

"What are you going to say to fans when they ask about [his latest arrest]?" she asked. "I'm going to say, 'I feel good! Papa's got a brand new bag and it's a man's word,'" he said, raising his voice. Then he stood and gyrated, shouting, "I FEEL GOOD!"

The interviewer decided enough was enough and attempted to end the interview, but Dad objected. "But I just got here! And I love you! I love America! I love everybody!"

She tried one final time for a substantive answer. "You're not troubled by all this [bad publicity]?" Dad laughed like a hyena and started to sing: "This is a man's world!" More than twenty-five years later, I still haven't been able to watch the entire interview. It hurts too much. I have read the comments from people, about Dad being "coked up," "pathetic," and "roasted." Most people think the interview is funny. I think it's sad and embarrassing.

Mom did her best to shield Deanna and me from the embarrassing publicity, and she tried her best to keep our life as normal as possible at home. Every time I was around Dad and Adrienne, I felt as if I was on a raft in troubled water. *Don't rock the boat, Yamma,* I would tell myself, *or someone might get hurt. And your friends will all read about in the tabloids.*

On the day after Easter in 1987, six weeks before I was scheduled to arrive for my summer visit, Dad got himself into hot water again. After a particularly ugly confrontation, Adrienne called the police and said my father had tried to kill her. I couldn't believe it. I knew they had a troubled marriage, but kill her? Dad was hauled into police headquarters and charged with attempted murder. *People* magazine got the lowdown when Adrienne invited them into their home. The story left little to the imagination about what went on behind the locked gates of the Brown estate.

"REAL MEN DON'T HIT WOMEN!" the story began. "So reads a series of billboards displayed around Beech Island, SC, the small town that soul superstar James Brown calls home. Unfortunately, Beech Island's most famous citizen may not have gotten the message."

I wanted to die.

The story goes on to describe how Dad had terrorized Adrienne, firing a rifle at her car (with her in it) and beating her with a metal mop handle. She'd been admitted to the hospital with black and blue marks all over her body. Adrienne told the magazine that Dad had beaten her other times—but only twice where it was bad enough that he knocked her teeth out. She claimed my father had guns he used to scare her, and that he would shoot up the house during arguments.

Of course, Dad's attorneys weighed in, claiming that both Dad and Adrienne had contributed to the stormy relationship and that was what made them such an "exciting couple." I'm glad he thought so. I was just a teenage girl, and having to deal with everyone knowing such intimate and embarrassing details of my father's life shook my world.

Hearing Adrienne's stories brought back memories of my father's treatment of my mother, memories I had chosen to forget. I began to feel a real disconnect from my dad. Part of me still loved being James Brown's daughter and sharing the perks of his privileged lifestyle, but the other part was mortified that my father was imploding for the entire world to see. I loved him so much and I idolized him, but I was starting to wish that no one knew he was my father. I wasn't mature enough to handle such complex emotions. On the outside I acted as if nothing were wrong, but I spent a lot of time in my room alone, hiding, hoping no one else was reading the stories that were out there, hoping Dad would come to his senses and stop shaming himself and us. I thought maybe being around me and Deanna would help Dad to settle down, but things just got worse.

I had just started my sophomore year when, on September 24, 1988, Dad took police on a high-speed chase through two states. Adrienne told reporters that Dad was on medication for jaw surgery and was "not in his right mind" when he tried to elude the police that day. Talk about enabling. The only medication he was on was angel dust. It seemed that Dad and Adrienne shared an appetite for the drug. I remember once picking up a newspaper and reading about their madness and then crying myself to sleep. The newspaper story gave details I didn't know about the September fiasco. It said that Dad had been in his office in Augusta on a Saturday and became enraged when he discovered that someone had used his private bathroom. So what did he do? He picked up a shotgun he just happened to have handy and went to the building next door, where an insurance seminar was going on. Swinging the shotgun around, he began ranting about the invasion of his privacy and demanded to know who had used his bathroom. The police were called and Dad took off in his truck. He was arrested after a chase that ended when the officers shot out his tires. A drug test showed PCP in his system. What a mess. I imagined if my sister and I had been there when all this was going on. The instability at their home was not a place for kids. I thank God for my mom and her strength to give us a more stable upbringing.

That year, Dad went to trial. His headline-grabbing performance would get him six years in prison and a new title: Inmate number 155413. Adrienne sold her story about living in an abusive relationship with my father—complete with photographs of her bruised and battered face—to the *National Enquirer*. I didn't care who was at fault. A big part of my world was shattering, and I was angry and scared. It's one thing to try to deal with a difficult family problem. It's really weird to see your family problems play out in a supermarket tabloid. I heard the whispers at school, especially when they grew louder and some mean girls began hissing "Free James Brown!" when they passed me in the hallways. They weren't being kind. Most kids could keep their family secrets hidden behind closed doors. Ours were being broadcast on CNN. So Dad had a dark side and now there was no denying it. I wasn't just upset that my father was a convict; I was horrified that the whole world knew about it.

I went to see my father twice when he was in prison. Adrienne went back and forth every week, and she took me along when I visited for the summer. She'd pack a cooler with sandwiches or chicken and drive Dad's van an hour and a half to the prison in Columbia, South Carolina. We never went inside. He always came out to us, and we'd sit in the van, eating our picnic lunch and making small talk. Then she'd take one of his famous black and silver combs out of her handbag and style his hair. I hated seeing my father in prison, but he was always in good spirits and he and Adrienne seemed to be getting along well while he was there.

Absence makes the heart grow fonder and all that.

10

Home from Jail

"There is no real reality to a really imagined life anymore."
—*Gertrude Stein,* The Geographical History of America

DAD CAME HOME in February 1991, after serving twenty-six months of his six-year sentence. All of the papers covered it and my father played it for all it was worth, shouting "I feel good!" to the throngs of reporters covering his release from prison. Regular reports followed about the clean and sober James Brown and how he had been rehabilitated in prison and was ready to resume his career. I figured that prison had been one of the best things to happen to him. He'd taken advantage of his time behind bars to get himself together.

That same summer, the summer before I went off to college, I went to South Carolina to stay with Dad and Adrienne. In July, *Ebony* magazine ran a gushing cover story about Dad. It talked about how he had made the best of a bad situation while he was in prison, how he rose at 3:30 every morning to work kitchen duty (ironic, because he always said cooking was for women), helped with the prison choir, and sometimes performed for his fellow inmates. The story said that, at one point during his prison stay, he became so distraught that he nearly cut off his prized, permed hair. Adrienne sustained him, Dad told the writer. She traveled four hundred miles every week to visit him and style his hair. (He slept in sponge rollers that the prison barber provided to preserve his famous hairstyle.) "I held on for my wife's and my father's sake," he was quoted as saying. No mention of the kids, of course. Talk about feeling inconsequential. Dad claimed that his ordeal made him appreciate Adrienne more. Again, no mention of me. He also told the writer that he had committed himself to helping the younger men he met in prison. "I tried to shake them, make them understand that education was valuable," he said of the youths he advised. "I thought if they heard it from the Godfather, maybe they'll stay away from drugs and get an education." Nice story, but it became evident pretty quickly that the Godfather wasn't practicing what he was preaching.

One day, I was hanging out with Adrienne at the house. Everything had been going well to that point and I was enjoying my summer in Beech Island. Dad had left for the office early that morning, and it was dark already when we heard his prized Lincoln roaring back up the driveway. He burst through the front door, his eyes blazing, his body sweating profusely. He started shouting at Adrienne, *"Give me the money! Give me the money!"* Right after Dad got out of jail he had signed on with Butch Lewis Productions to perform the pay-per-view concert "James Brown: Living in America." Butch was a legendary boxing promoter and he was Dad's good friend. He threw a party for Dad when he was released from prison and was helping him to get his career back on track. The pay-per-view concert had been a smashing success. That day, Dad learned that Adrienne, in her capacity as executive producer of the show, had collected a pile of money from the production that she was hiding

from him. Dad had already experienced business associates stealing money, and he was always paranoid about it. But this was his
wife! He didn't know that she had safely tucked the money away
in a safe.

I had heard Dad's rage plenty of times, but in my eighteen
years I'd never seen him like that, not even the time I saw him
beating up my mother. It was like there was a raging bull inside
of him and it was kicking to get out. I was terrified. I stood there,
frozen, afraid to speak. Adrienne was more afraid than I was, but
she began shouting back at Dad, calling him some of the worst
names I'd ever heard. "You're high," she screamed. "You're a no-
good motherfucker." I suddenly realized that Dad was tripping
out. Dad went back outside, and Adrienne ran to the door and
locked it behind him. A minute later, he was back again, banging
on the door, calling her names. "Bitch. Slut. Whore." I didn't know
what to do. Then he started calling out to me. "Yamma! Yamma,
come open the door!" Adrienne stared at me with a look that said,
Don't you dare. I looked from her to the door. Dad was still ranting
at me to open the goddamn door. I was afraid that if I pissed him
off, I'd get beat up. So what was I supposed to do, not let my father
into his own house?

I opened the front door and let him in. He was disheveled and
menacing. Adrienne came from behind me and slammed his money
down on the table. He picked up the cash, stormed off, and didn't
return until we were both sleeping. When I saw him again the following morning, it was as if nothing had happened.

"Good morning, Dad."

"Good morning, Yamma."

"Good morning, Adrienne."

"Good morning, Yamma."

"Good morning, Sugar."

"Good morning, Sugar Sugar."

It was a scene right out of *The Waltons*. I didn't understand the dynamics of this relationship or any married couple. I was still too young to understand.

11

Denzel

"Fame is the thirst of youth."
—Lord Byron, "Childe Harold's Pilgrimage"

I DON'T MEAN to imply that there weren't good times with Dad during that time. There were. And there were many moments still when I was proud to call him my father. One of those times happened in the summer of 1993. I was an undergraduate at the University of Maryland, and Dad had a date to play Wolf Trap in nearby Vienna, Virginia. He had just received a Lifetime Achievement Award at the Grammy Awards the previous year, and his post-prison career was soaring. I hadn't gone to Beech Island that summer, so when I heard he was coming to Virginia, I decided to drive up to see him. As usual, he allowed me to sit on the side of the stage to watch from there.

The concert was sold out, and Vice President Al Gore, who was a huge fan of Dad's, was in the front row. Dad invited Gore and his wife, Tipper, up on stage, and they happily obliged him. It was kind of surreal for me, watching the vice president of the United

States acting like a starstruck fan with my father. Dad called to me to come out on stage to join them. Now that was a moment, standing next to the vice president while he boogied (awkwardly) on center stage, surrounded by stone-faced Secret Service agents. The Gores were great, and I loved every minute of the concert. But for me, the real excitement began when it was over.

Dad was getting his hair rolled in his dressing room after the show, which was his routine. He always got all done up again after concerts, because he wanted to be well turned out for lingering fans. So he was in his curlers, under the dryer, when a knock came at the door and a man from Wolf Trap told me that Denzel Washington was waiting outside and wanted to meet Mr. Brown, if that was possible. Denzel was in town filming *The Pelican Brief* with Julia Roberts. I looked past the man from Wolf Trap and saw him standing there in a baseball cap and jeans. "Just a minute, please," I stuttered, then slammed the door and ran to Dad, nearly tripping over my own feet.

"Dad! Daaaaaad! Denzel Washington is outside and he wants to meet you!" I said, barely able to contain my glee.

Dad was nonchalant. "OK, Yamma," he said, adjusting one of his curlers. "Wait until I'm finished drying my hair and invite him in."

I was incredulous. *You're going to keep Denzel Washington waiting?* I wondered. "But what if he leaves before you're done?" I asked.

"He's not going anywhere," Dad replied.

"But . . ."

I grabbed my comb from my purse and fussed with my own hair. Denzel Washington was outside! *Oh my God!* I thought as I twisted a few strands of hair into place. *Denzel Washington!*

"What are you doing?" Dad asked, watching me smudge lipstick on my lips.

"I'm getting ready for Denzel!" I said.

Dad shook his head and chuckled. When he finished primping, he sent for Denzel. I prayed he was still there. I tried to act cool, but my face was burning. Then, after a moment, the door to the dressing room opened, and there he was.

"Hello, Mr. Brown," Denzel said, extending a hand toward my father. Oh that grin of his!

"Well hello, Mr. Washington," Dad replied, flashing his famous smile. Cool as a cucumber he was!

Denzel was the handsomest man I'd ever seen, but I was afraid to look at him for too long and get caught staring. He glanced from my dad to me and back to Dad.

"Please have a seat, Mr. Washington," Dad said.

"Are you sure?" Denzel asked. (*Are you kidding me?* I said to myself.)

"Mr. Washington, this is my daughter, Yamma."

"Nice to meet you, too, Yamma," he said.

"Nice to meet you, too," I said, tripping over my words and trying my best to be cool.

Dad and Denzel chitchatted for fifteen minutes or so. "Great concert, Mr. Brown. I've been a fan for a long time."

"Thank you, Mr. Washington."

I snuck as many glances as I could and tried not to giggle like a starstruck fool. I listened to every word without hearing much of what they were saying. I was too busy gaping and trying to act like I wasn't. Then, Denzel stood to leave.

"I don't want to keep you any longer," he said. "I know you're busy. But I'm in town filming and I heard you would be here. I wanted to make sure to come by and see your show and meet you."

"Glad you came, Mr. Washington," Dad said.

They shook hands again and Denzel was gone. I looked at the door as he closed it behind him, my mouth still agape. Dad shook his head from side to side.

That night, I drove back to Maryland reliving the moment over and over again. *Oh my God,* I said to myself. *That was Denzel Washington, and he was there to meet my Dad!* I could hardly wait to get back to the dorm to tell all of my friends.

Oh, and I'd have to remember to tell them that I'd danced on stage with the vice president, too. It was all so much fun and surreal. Then I went back to my normal life at the dorms to live the other of the two lives I led.

12

Adrienne's Dead

"Parting is all we know of heaven and all we need of hell."
—*Emily Dickinson, "Parting"*

THE NEXT TIME Dad was arrested for battering Adrienne was in December 1994. I was at college in Maryland when I heard about it on the news. The Aiken County sheriff's office had been called to the house on a domestic call. Adrienne told them that during a scuffle, my father shoved her to the floor and she hit a chair and split her lip. In March 1995 the charges were dropped because she refused to testify against Dad. He wrote her a note, which I found much later, after his death. It read:

Dear Adrienne,

This leaves me sad to write this, but after all is said and done, I know it's time that we go our separate ways. I can't love you anymore, even when I'm trying, when I think about you having me locked up three times. It's over. It can be done quietly or we can take it to the press, which is your thing."

True to his word, Dad filed for divorce (again), but soon they reconciled (again), and the fighting escalated (again). On Halloween night, 1995, Adrienne ended up in the hospital with a bloody nose and swollen and bleeding lips. She told the responding sheriff's deputies that Dad had hit her in the face. He was arrested and put in jail. *Extra! Read all about it!* My father denied beating Adrienne. He told the *Augusta Chronicle* that there was some kind of misunderstanding. He hadn't attacked Adrienne, as she claimed. He said he found her unconscious on the floor and when she came to, she asked why he'd hit her. He hadn't, he said; she must have been hallucinating. A week later, Adrienne signed an affidavit recanting her story of domestic abuse. Her injuries, she said, were caused when she accidentally bumped into a mirror in the house. Yeah, I thought, the same way my mom used to accidentally hit the wall.

Now, I'm not saying my father never laid a hand on Adrienne. I know better. But she wasn't the most credible witness. I knew my father beat her, but I never knew which of her stories were true. Miss Ella, who was still working for them, told me that Adrienne painted bruises on her face and arms for the photos that accompanied the *National Enquirer* story. I don't know if that's true or not. I do know that Miss Ella didn't lie. On the other hand, my father never owned up to his mess. It was always somebody else's fault. After that last domestic violence arrest, he told *Jet* magazine that Adrienne was responsible for all of their problems because she turned violent when she was high. "I love my wife," he said, "but I can't get her into a rehab clinic to stop her from abusing her prescription drugs." Talk about the pot calling the kettle black. If my father did try to get Adrienne help, I didn't know about it. I kept wishing for a happy ending.

And then it was too late.

Adrienne died on January 6, 1996. I was in pharmacy school in Atlanta, and my sister called me there to give me the news. Adrienne had gone in for liposuction surgery two days earlier and was recovering in a private care facility in Los Angeles when she collapsed and couldn't be revived. Besides the anesthesia left over from the surgery, a mixture of prescription painkillers and PCP was found in her system. Her heart had simply given out. She was forty-seven. Dad howled when the doctor called him at home in South Carolina. Miss Ella said he kept shouting, *"No! No! No! No!"* He told me he hadn't wanted Adrienne to get the surgery in the first place, but she'd insisted. I knew he would take her death hard.

Adrienne's passing was an excuse for the newspapers to regurgitate the stories of their marriage. What a sad way to be remembered: by your crazy, violent relationship with a crazy, violent famous man. Adrienne was so much more than my father's wife. But that's what made her newsworthy. And the news about her and him had been mostly bad.

My studies kept me from attending the private service for my stepmother in Hollywood Hills, but Deanna and I got to the second service, at the Imperial Theatre in Augusta. Mom came, too, but sat separately from Dad and us. It was the first funeral ever to be held in the historic theater, and every seat, from the orchestra section to the balcony, was taken. The glossy black casket was covered with a huge spray of red roses from Dad, and scores of other flower arrangements blanketed the stage. A large portrait of Adrienne was suspended over the casket, and a white cross was projected on the curtain at the back of the stage.

Among the eight hundred or so people who jammed into the theater were Rev. Sharpton and US Senator Strom Thurmond and his wife, Nancy, who was a close friend of Adrienne. Part of the service was in Hebrew because Adrienne was Jewish. It was a somber affair, the way funerals for people who were too young to die often are. Looking bereaved, Mrs. Thurmond gave a heartfelt tribute, saying Adrienne "devoted herself to helping James Brown continue leading the world as the Godfather of Soul. She was often on the lonely fringe throughout it all. She had a tremendous giving heart." Rev. Sharpton also spoke and he was eloquent as ever. Adrienne was one of the few people around Dad who didn't want anything from him "except to be James Brown," he said. Looking at Dad, he added, "Mr. Brown, you face a lonely time. Remember you have what most stars never have—someone who loves you."

The Rev. Reginald D. Simmons, who officiated, told us that he talked to Adrienne two days before she died, while she was recovering, and she was looking forward to coming home. When he spoke of the marriage, he alluded to problems. "God gave her a husband. Despite things down, up, or turned around, he was steadfast and unyielding," Simmons said. "Their relationship was going to be for better or for worse."

Dad chose not to speak but wrote something for the program. "Dear Adrienne," his message said, "Honey, my life will never be the same, wait for me. I want to be the first guest on your T.V. show in heaven. Yours always, James." I could tell how much Dad was hurting and it broke my heart. I was really worried that being alone might send him over the edge (if he wasn't already there). I told him that I loved him and that I was there for him, and he seemed to appreciate that. My father didn't cry in public, but I saw him tear up several times that day.

Adrienne was buried next to Dad's father in Walker Memorial Park in downtown Augusta. The silver plaque on her grave reads:

She was a native of Los Angeles, California, and the wife of "The Godfather of Soul," James Brown. She was a dedicated fighter for humanity, a lover of all people, a person who was not given the world on a silver platter but one who had to work very long and hard for everything she accomplished in life.

She was a diligent partner, a lady, a lover and a friend. Because of the love and affection she had for her father-in-law, Joseph "Pop" Brown, she requested to be buried next to him here in Augusta, to be joined by her husband James Brown and everyone in his family.

I will always have everlasting love for you and I will never forget you. I know one day we will meet each other again. . . . me, you, "Pop" and all of our family. We'll be together again forever. With tears in my eyes and pain in my heart, I say so long.

Your "Woggar" James.

I love you, Sugar!!!

Dad was sixty-two years old at that point, and he hadn't been without a companion for most of his adult life. He didn't like being alone. I imagined him padding around that big house not knowing what to do with himself. I wondered if he would be forced to take a good look at himself with no one there to deflect attention away from his demons. Did he understand that he was making a mess of his life? Did he realize that the way he treated women was wrong? Did he have the wherewithal to see himself for what he was beyond The Godfather of Soul—a wife beater and drug abuser? This I knew: Adrienne's death was either going to mean the further downfall of my father or it would be his wake-up call.

I prayed for the best and braced myself for the worst.

13

A Doctor in the House

"Learning is not attained by chance, it must be sought for with ardor and attended to with diligence."
—Abigail Adams in a letter to John Quincy Adams, May 1780

MY GRADUATION FROM pharmacy school in May 1997 was the proudest moment of my life, and it ranked right up there for Dad, too. My father never went past the seventh grade, so having a doctor in the family was something he could have never imagined when he was running barefoot on the streets of the Terry. Years earlier, I had wisely realized that my father's footsteps were too big and too deep for me to follow in them without falling on my face. I loved music and the entertainment business, but I was relatively young when I decided to pursue something different. My first time in a recording studio was the last time I ever dreamed of being an entertainer. I had a love for music; I had grown up with it. But standing next to my father and witnessing what it actually took to be James Brown—the superhuman energy, the God-given talent, and the intense pressure of it all—I realized there was no way in hell I wanted to be a performer. My passion wasn't deep enough and my talent wasn't great enough for me to stand up to the scrutiny of being my father's daughter in the entertainment business. Later in life, I would see what Lisa Marie went through, living in Elvis's iconic shadow, and I was ever grateful for that early awakening. I decided that I would be successful but on my own terms.

I'm sure the fact that Dad had a keen interest in medicine and a general admiration for people who worked in the medical field had something to do with my decision to become a pharmacist. I was the first in the family to earn my doctorate, and that was a really big deal. That advanced degree added a layer of closeness with my father. I wasn't just his daughter anymore; in his eyes a PhD meant you were a medical doctor. I was now someone who could talk to him about medical maladies and listen to him about his health concerns. It made me feel good that I wasn't just taking from Dad anymore. I could give something back.

Dad had always pushed the importance of education with us and with all young people. That didn't mean he was willing to pay for everything, though. He paid for my undergraduate education, but he was also a staunch believer in making your own way so I was on my own after that. When I told him I planned to pursue advanced degrees, he said, "You guys were born with silver spoons in your mouths. You need to understand what hard work is and to appreciate it." It went back to his song, "I Don't Want Nobody to Give Me Nothing." "I made it myself, and you can, too," he said. Still, for a long time I was certain that when all was said and done, he'd hand me a check for $100,000 and tell me to pay off my student loans. That never happened, and I discovered that his lesson was indeed the best gift he could have given me. The pride I felt in myself for doing things my way and myself were worth more than anything money could buy.

I had chosen to attend pharmacy school in Georgia to be closer to my father. He visited me there only twice, once for my pre-admission interview and again at graduation. Both times turned into James Brown stories. I was an above-average student in college, earning As and Bs. But that wasn't good enough to guarantee my admittance to pharmacy school. Aside from doing extra work, one of the stipulations of my acceptance was an interview with the dean. Dad decided he wanted to be there, even if it meant he sat outside in the waiting room. I have to think that was his way of helping me get into the program. *Look who her father is! It's none other than The Godfather of Soul himself!*

Well, Dad walked into the office with me, and I wish I had a picture of the dean's face. His eyes got like saucers and his mouth dropped open. It's not every day that James Brown shows up at your workplace. The dean looked as if he'd seen a ghost. Or a superstar. *Am I really standing here looking at James Brown?* Needless to say, the first part of the interview was all about Dad. The truth is, I couldn't have been more proud. The dean was a huge James Brown fan. He told Dad how much he admired him and his work. Dad basked in the praise, but after only a few minutes, he excused himself. "I'll wait for you out in the waiting room, Yamma," he said. I knew that he'd accomplished what he'd come for, to give me what he thought would be a leg up. Now he wanted me to have my time to shine. I felt so loved by it.

Fast-forward four years to graduation. Dad just happened to be home and not on tour at the time. I never expected that his schedule would allow him to be there, so when he told me he was coming I was beside myself with joy. Of course, we had to let the school officials know. He was James Brown after all, and chances were his presence would cause a bit of a stir.

Dad looked so handsome in a custom charcoal suit with black trim over a black shirt. He wore his signature pinkie ring with a *B* in diamonds and his favorite turquoise bracelet with his initials. I marveled at how young he looked. He never looked his age. Adrienne had been gone a year, and I knew that Dad had his ups and downs, but this was a good day. When his son Teddy, from his first marriage, died in a car crash, Dad threw himself into work. Adrienne's death was different; it paralyzed him. He didn't work at all for months, and he stayed hidden behind the walls of the Beech Island estate. Everyone was worried. I didn't know what to expect that day, but he came to the ceremony sober. He actually looked happy. I was both relieved and grateful.

Dad had tears in his eyes when I got my diploma. I'd only ever seen him cry once, when Adrienne died, so it was quite a surprise to see him wiping away tears. I was grateful for the moment. I really got to see—physically see—how he felt about my big accomplishment. He was just bursting with pride.

Dad was all about letting me shine that day. As hard as he tried to stay in the background, he couldn't control everything. After all, he was James Brown. To think that he would go unnoticed was just plain silly. I saw plenty of people glance his way that afternoon, but few approached him. They seemed to understand that this was a private family moment. That was, until the end of the ceremony.

We had planned a graduation celebration at Ray's on the River in Atlanta. As we waited in our limo to head off to Ray's, I noticed a white-haired man breathlessly approaching the car. He was animated, talking excitedly to our driver, who was standing outside. I couldn't hear what he was saying because the windows were closed and the air-conditioning was running, but our driver was soon beckoning Dad. "Excuse me, Mr. Brown," he said. "But this gentleman would like to meet you." Dad obliged, of course. He got out of the car and I saw him shake the man's hand. I watched as they talked. The man was absolutely besotted with my father. "Who was that?" I asked when Dad returned to the car. "It was the president of the university," he replied. I had just graduated from the school, but the president couldn't be bothered even to nod at me. It was one of those moments when reality sets in. Yes, Yamma, you got our doctorate degree. Yes, that's a big deal. But your father is James Brown, and the Godfather of Soul trumps everyone and everything. At that moment it was I who was filled with pride. I had my diploma, and the university president had Dad's autograph.

The party at Ray's couldn't have been better. I love the pictures from that day. Forty friends and family members gathered in a perfect spot overlooking the Chattahoochee River. All of Dad's children were there—me, Deanna, and all of our half brothers and sisters. Dad was seated at the head of the table. I looked into his eyes and could read his thoughts. This is what he had worked for: a thriving, happy family. And for that brief moment in time, the Browns really were.

Mom and Dad got along great that day. There was such ease about them when they were together. Both were single at the time, and I found myself wishing they would get back together.

And it almost happened.

Dad tried winning Mom back after that. He called her until she finally agreed to a date, and after that they began seeing each other again. They were really going to try to make it work. I was there when Dad apologized to Mom for the way he treated her during their marriage. My mom isn't one to hold grudges, and I knew she still loved my dad. In spite of myself, I conveniently pushed aside those terrible memories from the past and hoped for reconciliation. What child doesn't want her parents together, no matter her age?

Ultimately, my mom decided she couldn't go back. It had been one thing to have to deal with the other women, she told my father. "It wasn't that that drove me away. It was you beating me up." My father had the strangest response, one that I will never forget. He told my mother that she should have stayed and endured the beatings. "I would have learned my lesson eventually," he said. "I would have grown out of it." That was sad on so many levels. For him. For her. For us. First of all, he never outgrew his propensity for mistreating women. My father was raised in a culture of abuse. It was what men in his circles did. They didn't talk things out. Their attitude was, "I'm the man. I make the rules. I'm going to smack you so you don't talk back the next time." Of course it wasn't OK. But that was what he knew, and we all suffered for it.

Believe it or not, I was angry at my mother for not reconciling with Dad. I know that sounds strange, and I know that nothing would have changed from the first time they were together, but my overwhelming desire for a united family trumped my better judgment. Mom took the brunt of so much of my anger when, really, so much of that anger was at my dad.

Years later, I would witness that same kind of confused thinking from my own daughter when her father was abusing me.

14

Committing Dad

*"I have absolutely no pleasure in the stimulants in which I
sometimes so madly indulge. It has not been in the pursuit of
pleasure that I have periled life and reputation and reason.
It has been the desperate attempt to escape from torturing
memories, from a sense of insupportable loneliness,
and a dread of some strange impending doom."*
—*Edgar Allen Poe*

THE HAPPINESS I felt at my graduation, from seeing my father
look so healthy and seem so content, quickly faded. Dad began
turning up in public, clearly out of control. Having a parent who is
addicted is hard enough, but when that parent is a celebrity, you're
not just dealing with the addiction but also the embarrassment that
comes with the whole world knowing about it. Dad wore colored
glasses when he was high. He had them in all colors: yellow and
green and red. I called them his psychedelic glasses. He wore them
to hide his glassy eyes. I had seen him interviewed on TV on several occasions around that time and he was always wearing them.

I'd sit there in front of the television, wringing my hands and wishing for a quick ending. It really was like rubbernecking during a car crash. You're terrified to see what happened, but you can't make yourself look away. Every time he showed up on TV with those glasses on I'd think to myself, *Oh boy, here we go again. I hope this is over quickly, because it isn't going to end well.* I was in an emotional tug-of-war with myself. I was angry at him for his weakness and at the same time feeling guilty about being embarrassed by his behavior.

Just as I had feared, Adrienne's death had started a long, agonizing spiral downward for Dad. He would get better for a while and then relapse again. After each of Dad's public displays, people would look at me strangely, and I knew what they were thinking: "What's wrong with your father?" "What is he *on?*" I didn't have an answer. I should say I didn't *want* to answer. I knew that he was abusing drugs, but he was still my father and I felt as if I needed to protect him and his image. I used to loathe it when kids who admired him saw him high. Here he was, telling them to keep their lives on track, and he was a train wreck.

I have to be truthful. I was getting pretty tired of his craziness. The media poked fun at his antics, but I didn't see anything funny at all about what he was doing. I hate to say this, but I was losing respect for him. My father was a music genius who came from nothing and worked his way to the top of an industry that is notoriously difficult and cutthroat. He was so strong in so many ways. I'd look at him and think, *How could you be so weak to let a lousy street drug take over your life?* I never said it out loud. You didn't talk that way to my father. He would have considered it disrespectful, and I was afraid he would get angry and push me out of his life. Dad was the kind of person who always had to be right, and because he was a celebrity, people always yielded to him. I was no different. I had missed so much time with my father when I was a child and didn't want to lose him again, so I kept my mouth shut. Sometimes I had to clench my teeth to stop from speaking my mind. My hopes would rise when Dad seemed to be getting better, and then he would disappoint me once again. It tore me up to see him out of control, strung out, repulsive. And then, because of who he was—a man people looked up to, whom kids respected—I felt embarrassed for him. And embarrassed for me, too. I didn't know what to do besides wait for the inevitable crash.

It came in January 1998, just after the two-year anniversary of Adrienne's passing. My sister got a call from Miss Ella, who was still loyal to Dad and still working for him. She told Deanna that when she got to work that day she found my father buck naked except for the flag from my grandfather's coffin, which he had wrapped around himself. (Thank goodness the press didn't get a hold of that juicy detail.) His father had died a couple of years before Adrienne. With both of them gone, he told Miss Ella, he had nothing to live for. Dad was higher than a kite. He wasn't just incoherent and garbled. He was PCP-insane. Miss Ella was frightened. I would have been, too.

Deanna called me to fill me in. She thought we needed to intervene and get Dad the help he needed, with or without his consent.

"What should we do?" she asked.

"The only thing we can do," I said. "We want our father to live."

We got a court order and had Dad committed that same day. I was on the phone with Deanna while it was happening. We knew that Dad wouldn't go easily. I felt so guilty, having my sister go through that by herself, but I was too far away to get there in time for the intervention. There was quite a scene when the sheriff's officers drove up to the house with the order signed by the local magistrate. To say Dad was resistant about going with them is an understatement. He was furious.

The media got hold of the story right away, much to our chagrin. The Associated Press reported, "Brown, 64, known as the 'Godfather of Soul,' was picked up Thursday by deputies on a judge's order, according to a sheriff's report. The report listed the case as a 'mental transport.'" The story quoted Dad's agent as saying he'd become dependent on painkillers he was taking for a back injury. That was a good one. Buddy Dallas, Dad's attorney, took the charade a step further, telling the media that Dad had simply been resting in the hospital after a grueling concert schedule. "James is taking a long, well-deserved rest," Mr. Dallas said. "He's been touring for the past five years."

My father's so-called friends had done what they always did—made excuses for him. Of course they did; he was their gravy train, and they enabled him. They needed for him to get back to work and make money! And he paid them to lie.

Within a week, Dad was back home. The whole incident was just a "misunderstanding," he told the local paper. And Deanna was to blame. There was nothing wrong, Dad told the reporter from the *Augusta Chronicle*. He wasn't having a mental breakdown. He wasn't even hooked on painkillers, as his agent had publicly claimed. "My daughter made a mistake," he said. "She should have just called me and asked if she could come over and check on me, but she called the police. Then they came and asked me if I would go to the hospital, and I didn't want to say no." Talk about spinning the truth!

Dad didn't speak to Deanna or me for weeks afterward. I don't think he ever completely forgave us.

15

Prince Charming

"Nothing in this world was more difficult than love."
—*Gabriel Garcia Márquez*, Love in the Time of Cholera

AROUND THAT SAME time, I began dating my future husband, Darren Lumar. I was working clinical rotations at DeKalb Medical Center in Atlanta and was the resident pharmacist on the medical team caring for his stepfather. You couldn't miss Darren. He was a bear of a man at six feet, five inches tall and 280 pounds. He was also charismatic and smart. And he was a real flirt. "Oh you look so cute in your lab coat!" he'd say. "Please don't tell me you have a boyfriend!" At first, I stuck to conversations about his stepfather's heart meds. But the more he talked, the more interested I became in him. He said he was an investment banker with his own international company and that he had played professional baseball for the New York Mets. He was well educated, an honors student who had earned his undergraduate degree at Loyola University in New Orleans and pledged Kappa Alpha Psi at Tulane. When he asked me to dinner, I accepted. That was February 1998.

I didn't tell Darren who my father was. Not at first. I didn't need another person using me for my namesake. A couple of months into the relationship, when I finally did fess up, Darren acted as if he had no idea my father was James Brown.

"No!"

"Yes."

"No way."

"Really, yes."

"Really?"

"Yes!"

Things between Darren and I moved fast after that. After dating for just two months, we went to Beech Island to visit Dad that April. To my surprise, Darren asked Dad for my hand in marriage. That was before he even asked me! I thought it was kind of old-fashioned but sweet. Dad was impressed by Darren's success. I think he was relieved that I wasn't with some freeloader who was more interested in his bank account than his daughter. "If you're happy, Yamma, then I'm happy," Dad said. A month later, I was formally engaged. It happened on Mother's Day. Darren and I were out to lunch with both of our mothers when he dropped to one knee and proposed. "I can't imagine my life with anyone but you," he said. Everyone was shocked, and I hadn't expected the proposal that day, either. I didn't hesitate with my answer. "Yes!" I said. "Yes!" I was overjoyed at the prospect of spending my life with Darren. But within just a few weeks, I would see a side of him that frightened me: an angry, aggressive side that seemed to come out of nowhere.

We had just moved in together in a luxury high-rise in Atlanta. We had the normal adjustment problems, bickering over things like where pictures should be hung and how to arrange the sofa in the living room. Living with someone is so different from dating. I quickly noticed that Darren was quite jealous. I could sense him tense up when I said hello to the doorman or came home a few minutes later than I said I would.

One day, I had planned to go shopping for things for our new place, but Darren, for reasons I have never known, decided I must have been going to meet a man. He started arguing with me about leaving the apartment. I was stunned by his belligerence. I was just going shopping, for goodness' sake. He was convinced otherwise. I couldn't reason with him. I tried walking away from him, but he wouldn't let up. He followed me around the apartment, pushing his finger in my face, calling me stupid and worse. When I'd had enough, I picked up my car keys and headed for the door. "I'm going shopping," I said.

Darren followed me from the apartment into the hallway. He followed me into the elevator, still ranting like a madman. "OK, Darren," I said, trying to sound calm. "Enough. We had our argument; now let's cool off." Darren wouldn't let it go. He was all up in my face. I was really scared. The elevator stopped at the lobby and I walked off and headed out of the building to my car. Darren was on my heels, still cursing and shouting. *"Bitch! Slut! Whore!"* When I finally got to my car, he grabbed my keys from my hand and threw them to the ground. I bent down to pick them up, and he pushed me to the pavement. I would get in the car when he was finished talking, he said, not before. Did I understand? "OK," I said. I tried getting up. He pushed me down again. I finally picked myself up and headed toward the busy street. Darren stalked me to the road, still screaming at me. No one stopped to help, and I'm pretty sure I would have waved anyone away had they tried. "Leave me alone!" I cried. "I don't want to argue with you!" I should have run and never looked back. But I didn't. God knows why. We headed back up to the apartment, where Darren eventually cooled down and then apologized.

He was so sorry, he said. He never meant to hurt me. It was just that he was under so much stress. He didn't know what to do with his frustration. It would never happen again, he promised. I was his princess, and going forward, he would never again forget to honor and respect me as much as he loved me.

"OK," I said.

Why hadn't I run and kept running? Probably for the same reason that my mom stayed with my father for as long as she did.

In her book, *It's My Life Now*, Meg Kennedy Dugan wrote:

> There were probably many factors that kept the relationship going and kept your love alive. There were all his promises. "I promise this will never happen again." You believed him the first time. And the second. As the abuse continued, he became increasingly remorseful, his promises more insistent. You continued to believe him; you wanted to believe him. After all, you loved him.

And that's what I told myself when I made the decision to stay with Darren. I loved him.

16

Meet Tomi Rae

"Beauty is in the eye of the gazer."
—Charlotte Brontë, Jane Eyre

DAD WAS IN rehearsals for his show at the legendary House of Blues at the Mandalay Bay Resort and Casino on the strip in Las Vegas when I decided to fly there to spend his sixty-fifth birthday with him. Little did I know when I boarded the plane in Atlanta that I was the one who was about to get a big surprise. Dad had a new girlfriend. Her name was Tomi Rae Hynie. I'll admit it, when I first laid eyes on her I thought to myself, *Dad, are you serious? You're dating white trash.* There are plenty of stories out there about when and how Dad and Tomi Rae got together. Years afterward, she told Larry King in a interview on CNN that they met when she auditioned to be a backup singer for Dad. At the time, she said, she'd been scratching out a living as a Janis Joplin impersonator in small clubs in Vegas. She jumped at the chance to audition for James Brown. He'd hired her on the spot and their relationship quickly became physical, she said.

"How long did you wait?" King asked.

"We waited three nights," Tomi Rae replied.

That was too much information for me.

When I got to Las Vegas and checked in with Dad at rehearsal, Tomi Rae was with him. He introduced her as one of his backup singers. I could see he liked her. I admit I was stunned. Tomi Rae was young—very young. She was nearly forty years Dad's junior, although she looked as if she'd lived a lot in her short life. Tomi Rae apparently had a rough childhood. She ran away from home at the age of fourteen, eventually landing in Las Vegas, where she formed an all-girl band she named Hardly Dangerous. When the band split, she got the Janis Joplin gig on the strip. She looked like a groupie, and she acted that way, too. She was unrefined and rough around the edges. Her clothes were tacky and her teeth were bad. I thought to myself, *OK. This has got to be a fling. He can't be serious.* But then I thought, *I know how he is. He's all about taking someone and fixing her up. He's going to totally change her.* He would buy her the right clothes, have her breasts enhanced, get her teeth fixed. He'd teach her how to look the way he wanted her to look, be the way he wanted her to be.

He had his work cut out for him.

Dad told me that it would make him happy if I'd hang out with Tomi Rae while I was there. He wanted us to get to know each other. He asked me to take her shopping and he gave her money to splurge. Rather than heading for the shopping district, though, Dad's new girl took me to a bar in the bowels of the city, somewhere off the beaten path. It was where she hung out with her rock 'n' roll buddies. Everyone at the bar knew her. We sat down and she lit a cigarette, and even though it was the middle of the day, she ordered shots for the bar. I thought, *Aren't we supposed to be shopping? Does my Dad know you're doing this?*

For the next couple of hours, Tomi Rae drank shots and talked about my dad. She raved about how talented he was and how excited she was to be singing on stage with him. Years later, in an interview with freelance writer Charles Thomson, she said she fell in love with Dad after "witnessing his dynamism and charisma onstage." Tomi Rae told me that she had struggled with drugs, which worried me, and said she'd been in and out of rehab in the past. She also complained to me about Dad's controlling nature and she asked if he had always been that way. "Yeah," I said. "Get used to it." I couldn't help but think about Dad's relationship with Adrienne.

I never thought Tomi Rae would be in our lives for any length of time. Dad had been doing really well. His bizarre behavior had subsided, and he seemed on solid ground. I hoped he wouldn't want to be in another serious relationship with someone who was on drugs. Tomi Rae was nice enough, but she certainly wasn't someone I could look up to or respect as my dad's future wife. But I did have to treat her respectfully. Dad was the type of person who had the attitude, "This is the one who I'm with. I don't care if you like her, but you have to show her respect." In his mind, that meant addressing her properly, the way he insisted we address all of his girlfriends and the way he wanted people to address him. For instance, one of his girlfriends after he and my mom parted was named Gloria. We were expected to call her Miss Daniels or Auntie Gloria, never just Gloria. I always obliged. Not when it came to Tomi Rae, though. No way was I going to call her Miss Hynie or, oh my goodness, *Auntie Tomi*. I couldn't have kept a straight face. I wasn't a kid anymore, and in any case she was only a couple of years older than I was. So I called her Tomi Rae. Dad didn't correct me. Somehow, he just knew better.

17

A Baby and a Wedding

*"Family faces are magic mirrors. Looking at people who belong
to us, we see the past, present, and future."*

—*Gail Lumet Buckley*

SHORTLY AFTER I returned home from Las Vegas, I learned I was
pregnant. It was unplanned, and to tell you the truth, I was shocked
and a little bit scared. Darren's angry outbursts had abated some
after that terrible incident when he pushed me to the ground in the
parking lot of our apartment building. Occasionally, he still shoved
me or wagged his finger in my face and called me names, but then
he'd calm down and all would be forgotten. I hoped that a baby
would mean the end of his bad behavior.

Darren was thrilled about the prospect of having a baby. We
did what most expectant parents do. We bandied about names and
bought furniture for a nursery. We shopped for baby clothes and
watched my stomach grow. In the middle of my pregnancy, Darren
decided we needed more room to accommodate a child, so we moved
from our high-rise apartment to a house in the Atlanta suburbs.

Darren went with me to each of my doctor's appointments. He was really supportive at times. When things were about to go bad again, when I could see he was becoming irritable or annoyed about something, I was able to sense it and I did what I could to avert his physical punishment. I needed to protect myself, but mostly I needed to protect my unborn child. We still had frequent arguments, but there was always a makeup period when he'd send me flowers or write me poetry and tell me how sorry he was. Each time I told myself that it would be the last time. I knew in my heart that things could have been better, but I wanted to fight to make my marriage work. I felt there was honor in standing by your man. I told myself we just needed time. Eventually everything would work out. I had learned my childhood lessons well.

My pregnancy was complicated, so much so that I was on bed rest for the last month or so. I had to give up my big salary to go on disability, which meant we were going to struggle financially for a while. Darren did not have a nine-to-five job with a regular salary. He earned commission for putting together business deals for other people and then recruited investors to fund the various projects. He could go months between big paydays and often did. So we lived on much less money while we waited for the baby to be born.

If he was stressed by the shortage of funds, he didn't show it. He was a doting husband. He made sure my breakfast was made before he left for the office, and he left a cooler of sandwiches by my bed so I wouldn't have to get up to make myself lunch. He even wrote me poetry. It was a period when Darren shined. I thought it was because he felt protective of our child and me. But looking back, I now realize that he was in better spirits because he wasn't anxious all the time, worrying about where I was, whom I was with, and what I was doing. I was stuck at home, barely able to leave my bedroom. What was there to fret about? There wasn't a moment in a day when he couldn't account for me. He was in complete control.

Our daughter, Sydney, was born on April 15, 1999. We had planned to be married by then, but time passed quickly, and, with the difficult pregnancy and time off for bed rest, it just never happened. Darren was in love with our daughter. He was a natural father. My disability funds were declining, so when the baby was a month old, I went back to my job as a hospital pharmacist. I took the night shift at the hospital, and Darren had night duty at home.

Those were some of our happiest days together, but it was also when I began noticing little inconsistencies in the stories Darren told me. I began to suspect that some of his biography was fabricated. He said he had an undergraduate and master's degree, yet he could never produce a diploma from either of the schools he said he'd attended. The biggest doubt I had was his claim that he'd played for the Mets. I had always been a little bit skeptical of that story. I checked it out and discovered he wasn't listed on any of the rosters during the years he said he played for them. When I asked him why, he amended his original story and said that he played pro ball only during the 1995 Major League Baseball strike. He went back to the minors after that and then decided to change careers. You know how hard we try to convince ourselves otherwise when someone we love seems to be lying? I tried telling myself things like I had misheard Darren when he told me his initial story. Or maybe I just plain got it wrong. But as hard as I tried to come up with excuses for him, I couldn't quell my growing mistrust.

I confided my doubts about Darren's truthfulness to my sister—and also hinted at the abuse I'd suffered, telling her about the time he had pushed me in the parking lot. Deanna urged me to break off the engagement, but I wouldn't listen. I loved Darren. And breaking up isn't so easy when there's a baby in the picture.

So, instead, Darren and I set a wedding date: July 24 of that year. I planned a fairytale wedding with bridesmaids and groomsmen and two hundred invited guests. The ceremony was slated for the Hopewell Missionary Baptist Church in nearby Norcross, Georgia. Our three-month-old daughter would be present at the altar and be baptized at the same time. At that point, all that mattered was Darren and the baby and me. We were the family I'd always wanted.

The days leading up the wedding were filled with angst. Despite my happy smile, the second thoughts I had buried so deep were reemerging, and I wasn't sure I wanted to marry Darren at all. But I didn't see any way out. My sister had grudgingly agreed to be in the wedding, but I knew she was unhappy about it. Dad wasn't even sure he would make it because he was scheduled to perform in Woodstock, New York, that day.

On the night before the ceremony, we all piled into the church for the wedding rehearsal. All of the tensions had bubbled up and were about to boil over. The timing couldn't have been worse. The evening was a disaster. First, my sister refused to take her position at the altar. Darren knew there was a problem, but he didn't know what it was and it made him grumpy. I tried to be happy-go-lucky, hoping that everything would just settle down. It didn't. Deanna was nearly in tears. She told me I was making the biggest mistake of my life and she didn't want any part of the wedding. She couldn't condone the marriage. "He pushed you!" she cried. "He fabricates things. He isn't who you thought he was. He made up stories because he thought the only way he could get you interested in him was if he had money and success. You don't even know who the real Darren is. Why does he feel the need to represent himself as someone he isn't? What is his motive?"

Somewhere deep within me I knew she was saying that Darren was a fraud and that he was using me because of who I was. I was the daughter of James Brown. But it was the eve of my wedding. What did she want from me? What was I supposed to do? I had my doubts about marrying Darren, but I loved him and I had an infant. I stood my ground and lashed out at my sister. "You don't have to be here!" I cried. "If you don't like him, fine, but this is who I choose. You don't have to like it."

The argument escalated, with both of us saying things we shouldn't have. Deanna and I had never had a serious blowup before that day. "We've come this far," I finally said, trying to diffuse the situation. "You just need to accept it. If you can't be happy for us, then don't be in the wedding." Deanna turned and walked out of the church.

Needless to say, the rehearsal was over. I was crushed. I needed my sister with me. I needed her to buoy me up because I was terrified of the step I was about to take. I felt like a trapped rat. It was too late to turn back. I decided I was going to be married and I was going to be happy about it. At that point, I didn't want anyone's opinion. If you weren't with us, I wanted you out of the way. Darren and I ended up having a great evening with our friends. At the end of the dinner, I went back to our house with my bridesmaids, and he checked into a hotel with his groomsmen.

I woke up the next morning surrounded by friends, some of them from as far back as middle school, but I was feeling my sister's absence. It felt like a cloud over my head. My friends were worried, and there was a lot of second-guessing going on. "Are you sure this is what you want?" they asked. "This is what I want," I replied. My attendants and I spent the morning doing what girls do when they're dressing up. We got our hair and makeup done and had our nails manicured. Everyone loved my dress. It was white and floor-length and encrusted with jewels. I have to admit it: I looked fabulous. But as the time for the ceremony drew closer, I began to feel angry and sad. All I could think about was the argument with my sister and that my dad might not make it to my wedding. We always sacrificed for his fame. That was just the way my life had always been. But this was my wedding! Why couldn't I be his priority just this once? Why couldn't my sister have held her comments until another time? Why couldn't my dad see that I needed him more than ever before?

To top off my sour mood, I realized I'd locked my keys in my car. Darren was the only person with a spare key, so I had to call him at the hotel and ask him to come to the rescue. When he arrived at the house, I couldn't help myself. I thought, *This is an omen. The groom is not supposed to see the bride until she walks down the aisle.* Breaking the rule meant bad luck. I felt like shaking myself. *Why couldn't I allow myself even a moment of unchallenged happiness?* I asked myself. I had a choice: ruin the day or decide to make the best of it. At that moment, I disregarded all of my doubts and negative thoughts and vowed I would be a happy and hopeful bride.

When I got to the church I saw my sister waiting for me. She smiled and we embraced. "You look beautiful," she said. I could feel some of the stress leaving my body. We were going to be OK. I heard someone say that the father of the bride had arrived. Things were working out! I let out a huge sigh of relief. Dad had boarded a plane in New York at 5:30 that morning so that he was sure to make it to the late-afternoon church service and walk me down the aisle. Afterward, he would fly back to Woodstock in time for his next performance that same night.

Dad looked at me lovingly as we waited in the vestibule for the ceremony to begin. "It's still not too late, Yamma," he said. "You can always back out, you know. I will take you away with me and you won't have to face anyone." I took Dad's comments as a joke. I'll never know if he meant them that way or if he sensed that the situation wasn't quite right and was trying to give me an out. At that moment, I should have bolted like Julia Roberts in *Runaway Bride*. But I didn't. The organ started to play and I took my father's arm for the walk down the aisle. "No, Dad," I said. "I'm ready." He smiled and nodded. "OK, baby girl. OK."

It was a beautiful Christian wedding ceremony. Afterward, I changed into a flowing white chiffon gown for the reception at a local restaurant and then danced the night away with my new husband, family members, and friends. I felt like the luckiest girl in the world. My dad hadn't disappointed me, and my sister had come around. And, most important, my husband was acting like the good Darren. I couldn't have been happier or more in love that night. I was truly at peace.

Dad couldn't stay long. He had to catch his flight back to New York. Before he left for the airport, he shook Darren's hand. "Take care of my little girl," he said. Darren assured him that he would.

A month later, my new husband shoved me so hard I went flying across our bedroom and slammed into the wall.

18

Texas

"Part of every misery is, so to speak, the misery's shadow
or reflection: the fact that you don't merely suffer but have to
keep on thinking about the fact that you suffer. I not only live
each endless day in grief, but live each day thinking about
living each day in grief."

—C. S. Lewis, A Grief Observed

A FEW MONTHS after the wedding, I got a job offer I couldn't refuse, making six figures as a clinical pharmacy manager at a company based in Houston. Darren and I packed up our six-month-old daughter and moved to Texas. We bought a five-bedroom house in a golfing community in Sugar Land, an affluent suburb about thirty miles southwest of Houston. I worked during the day, and Darren stayed at home with Sydney and looked for a job. The mortgage on our house was huge, so money was tight with just me working, but the move was just what we needed. We could start over in a place where we didn't have to worry about interference from our families, and we could finally get to know each other as husband and wife.

It didn't take long for me to learn that a change of scenery wasn't an elixir for a sick marriage.

Darren and I still argued a lot. We usually fought over money. He handled the finances and he claimed he had plenty of money coming in from his business venture in Atlanta. But my salary was paying all of the bills, and there didn't seem to be much left over. He could never explain why the money was so tight. Also, Darren had a roving eye, and I began to suspect that he was seeing other women. Every time I did the laundry I found scraps of paper with phone numbers in his pockets. He often went outside to take calls on his cell phone. Whenever I tried to broach the subject of him cheating, he turned things around on me, accusing me of being jealous and insecure.

Our worst fight happened when we had been living in Texas for about six months. It was right before Sydney's first birthday in April 2000. I had her in my arms. I don't even remember why he was angry, but Darren pushed me so hard that he knocked the wind out of me. I went flying across the room. I held onto our daughter with every ounce of my strength and somehow managed to maneuver my body at the last second to miss slamming into the wall. I landed partially on the bed, still clutching my screaming toddler. Hurting me was one thing, but I never thought Darren would put our child in harm's way. I didn't know then what I know now: that in a third to more than half of homes where there is spousal violence, a child is also being abused.

I was beyond being frightened at that point. I was furious and crying out of sheer anguish. "I'm calling my father to tell him what a jerk you are!" I screamed. Darren admired my father. I thought if Dad told him to knock it off, to keep his damn paws off his little girl, Darren would think twice the next time he was tempted to manhandle me. I was sure my father's disapproval would make an impression on him. I don't think Darren believed I'd call Dad. He waved me off and stormed out of the room.

But I did call. As soon as Darren was gone, I picked up the phone and dialed my father. I was sobbing as I told him what happened. "Darren shoved me into a wall with the baby in my arms," I said. I told him that it hadn't been the first time he'd abused me. He had hurt me before, plenty of times. I hadn't wanted to say anything because I thought I could make it work, I explained. But this time had been too much. I was holding our baby. "I'm scared, Dad," I said. "I'm really, really scared."

My father listened quietly as I spoke. When I finally stopped crying, he began to speak. "Yamma," he said. "I love you both. Marriage is hard. Everyone has problems. Disagreements. You're no different than anyone else. Try to work it out. Don't call me again until you do."

To say I was stunned would be a huge understatement. I don't know what I wanted from my father or what I expected him to say, but it wasn't that. I put down the phone and sobbed. *How dare you!* I thought. *I'm telling you I'm being abused and you aren't even taking my side? You're my father! What is wrong with you?*

That conversation is something I have never been able to shake, no matter how much time passes, no matter how much I try to rationalize my father's reasons for giving me such heartless advice. I have never felt so disappointed. So betrayed. So utterly alone. I'd wanted my father to rescue me. I'd wished he'd be my knight in shining armor. Do you know what it took for me to make that call to him? To admit that my husband was an abuser and that, beginning before we were even married, he had pushed me, shoved me, slapped me, busted my lip, and called me the most terrible, demeaning names? Battered women are typically secretive about what is happening to them. It takes tremendous courage to finally tell. I'd imagined my father charging to my defense, getting on the phone with Darren and telling him, "Don't you lay a hand on my baby girl. Don't you dare!" Instead, he sent me back into the lion's den and told me not to bother him again until *I'd* made it better.

I have forgiven my father for many things but not what he said to me that night. Childbirth was less painful than that rejection. Looking back, I don't know why I was so surprised by his response. How could he condemn Darren for abusing me when he had done the same to every woman with whom he'd ever had a relationship? To concede to me that Darren's behavior was inexcusable and egregious would have been to admit his own failures, his own crimes. Talk about calling the kettle black, right? But did my father even think that what Darren had done was wrong? That is a question that most disturbs me and one for which I will never have the answer. My father was raised to think women had to know their place, and if that meant teaching them using physical punishment, then so be it. I suppose I thought the rules would be different when it came to his own daughter, but I was wrong.

I felt defeated after talking to my father. I did whatever I had to do to keep peace in my home, to keep from rocking the boat and upsetting my husband. Darren was all I had. I certainly couldn't count on my family for any kind of support. My only option was to do the hard work of trying to keep my precarious marriage on an even keel, just as my mother had tried to do years before. As always, things settled down between Darren and me. He brought me candy and flowers and promised to never push me around again.

Like I said, he had trouble telling the truth.

19

All in the Family

*"Things come apart so easily when they have been
held together with lies."*
—*Dorothy Allison,* Bastard Out of Carolina

IT TOOK NINE months, but Darren finally landed a job as the
head of a technology start-up called Hyperdynamics, an oil and
gas exploration company in Houston. The money was OK, around
$80,000 a year. The job was right up Darren's alley, finding inves-
tors for the company. The press release to announce the hire was
impressive but embellished:

> Darren-Anthony Lumar, age 30, became Executive Vice Presi-
> dent of Hyperdynamics Corporation on November 2, 2000.
> Lumar has a wealth of experience in investor relations, capital
> formation, relationship management, and due diligence compli-
> ance. As Vice President of Capital Acquisition for First Financial
> Services, LLC, Lumar successfully managed to secure financ-
> ing of over $30,000,000. Lumar also served as Vice Presi-
> dent of Capital Management for the Economic Planning and

Development Council. Lumar assisted in establishing financial management standards and practices for new venture start-ups as well as emerging growth companies. Most recently as President of Lumar Worldwide Consulting, Lumar assisted small to mid-sized companies in developing relationships necessary for proper capital formation and core business development. Mr. Lumar received a degree in Economics and a Masters of Business Administration from the University of Devonshire (London, England).

As I said earlier, I knew little about my husband's business ventures or how much money they brought in. I still don't know which of the many "accomplishments" listed in his biography were real and which were just plain fiction. What I do know is that the University of Devonshire is a diploma mill, and Darren's "degree" was a piece of paper he received after taking an online correspondence course. Although it sounded impressive, it meant nothing. It was as good as a fake degree. I suspect that most of what he claimed for the company press release was bull. But at least he was finally bringing in an income, which eased some of our fights over money.

I rarely saw my father during the time I lived in Texas. He was living in South Carolina with Tomi Rae, and I didn't have any interest in being involved in their lives. Tomi Rae always seemed to be in and out of rehab for her drug addiction. I didn't want anything to do with that world. I was focused on my own problems and didn't have time for the drama going on in their lives. If there was anything significant happening in South Carolina, Deanna, who lived three miles from Dad and Tomi Rae in Beech Island, would call to fill me in. When my sister did have news, it was usually something unsettling.

Like the time shortly after Darren got his new job that she called to say Tomi Rae was pregnant. I couldn't believe it. What was my father thinking? He was in his mid-sixties and suffering from diabetes, and Tomi Rae was a flake. I have to admit it really bothered me, so much so that, as soon as I heard, I called my father and asked if he was sure the baby was his. Everyone wanted to ask him the same question, but I was the only one with enough chutzpah to actually ask. I said, "You are James Brown. This woman could be pulling the wool over your eyes. Just so you know, there are tests to prove such things." Dad didn't seem fazed by my concern. He calmly said, no, he didn't intend to ask for testing to prove the paternity of the child. "I'm not going to do that to Tomi Rae," he said. "I trust her." When I heard that, I decided to leave it alone. Not long afterward, I learned I was pregnant again. I was going to have a child and a sibling who were the same age.

Tomi Rae gave birth to James Brown Jr. in June 2001. Our son, Carrington, was born three months later, in September. Just a couple of years ago, during an interview with Charles Thomson, Tomi Rae reflected on that time in her life with my father. She said Dad named the boy. "James thought his son might be president one day," she said. "When he named him he said, 'I gave him my name because I knew that having my name and being half white, he might actually have a shot in this world. He could become the president of the United States one day.' He said that this boy was going to do more than he ever did. I felt those shoes were too big to fill."

Tell me about it.

Deanna called again with more news right before Thanksgiving. "I have something to tell you," she said. "Dad and Tomi Rae are getting married." I took in a deep breath. "When?" I asked. "Next month," she said. An invitation to the celebration followed. The wedding was to take place on December 14, a private affair with one hundred or so guests, including the mayor of Augusta, at the

Beech Island house. I didn't go. I had a new baby and I was too wrapped up in my own worries. I told my father I was sorry that I couldn't make it. My sister would be there and she could take plenty of pictures and send them to me later, I said, which she did.

I don't know if he was disappointed. I couldn't tell. It didn't escape me that my father had gone to a lot of trouble to get to my wedding just a couple years earlier. But I just couldn't bring myself to go to his. I felt bad and tried to allay my guilt with excuses. *They decided around Thanksgiving to get married just before Christmas. They know I live in Texas. I have a full-time job, a toddler, and a three-month-old child. The holidays are a terrible time to travel, especially with a couple of small kids. Why should I drop everything in my life to go to a wedding when I was given only three weeks' notice?*

Deanna said the party was nice enough. Tomi Rae was dressed in a white satin gown with a long train, and both my dad and Little Man (his pet name for my half brother), who was just six months old, wore formal black tuxes. The guests dined on an elaborate buffet of shrimp, salmon, and steak. The most memorable moment of the night for most people had to be when Dad serenaded his new bride with the song "Time after Time." I enjoyed seeing the pictures, but I never regretted missing the wedding. I had better things to do—like trying to keep my threadbare marriage from unraveling completely.

Meanwhile, Darren started his own investment company. He called it Lumar Worldwide Industries. I didn't know much about the business, only that he put together projects with investors and took a commission. I did see documents he claimed were for his business deals, but I didn't understand the jargon. Rather than trying to interpret it, I simply signed on the line where Darren put his finger. Darren talked about things like oil pipelines in Africa and clothing lines with professional athletes. I usually half-listened.

Whatever he was doing, it seemed to be working. We suddenly had money to spend. We were living the high life and I liked it. Both of us had champagne tastes. I was buying designer shoes and Tiffany jewels. Darren wore Armani suits, and we had luxury cars parked in the driveway. My husband also seemed to have more time to be home with the kids. One day, I walked in on him sitting in front of the television screen with Carrington, who was by then a toddler, next to him. Both of them were sucking their thumbs. Yes, Darren was a thumb-sucker. I learned about it after we started dating and tried to break him of the habit, suggesting he chew gum or something—anything—but nothing worked. I cringe now just thinking about him sitting there with his finger in his mouth. There's nothing appealing about a grown man sucking on his thumb. To make matters even worse, I later learned that he occasionally sucked his thumb during business meetings.

Neither money nor his oral fixation did anything to assuage Darren's rage, though. He had a short fuse and he continued to act out—and not just with me. In 2002, he barged into the office of a business associate to start an argument about a deal gone bad and threatened to kill the man. I don't think he meant it literally. But he could be quite persuasive. He was big and bulky, and when he was mad, he'd get all up in your face and read you the riot act. For that little temper tantrum he was charged with terroristic threats and sentenced to community service, which he blew off. He told me—and apparently his probation officer at the time, according to an article in *Atlanta* magazine a couple years back—that he had no intention of fulfilling his punishments because it wouldn't look good for a successful investment banker to be "picking up trash on the road."

In the midst of that mess, Darren and I got into another argument over his womanizing. I questioned him about a phone number

I found in his pocket. He tried to wave me off again, but this time I dared to raise my voice. I hadn't even finished my sentence when he hauled off and popped me in the mouth. When I dialed 9-1-1, he wrestled the phone away from me, but the police came anyway. When they saw my bloody lip, they arrested him. I had to give his mother, Verna, bail money to get him out of jail. When she brought him home, she lectured me. "It's not right what he did," she said. "But you shouldn't have called the police and let them in on your business."

We went to court and I dropped the charges.

Things got worse after that. Darren and I tried couples therapy, but that didn't work. He continued to be moody and cruel, and I still found slips of paper with strange phone numbers jotted on them in his pants pockets. I also began to notice that he was embellishing the truth about even simple things. And then he embellished his lies. For instance, when he told new friends in Texas about his past, he didn't just say he played for the Mets. He now said he thought he would still be picked up by the Arizona Diamondbacks. I thought that was bizarre. I'd never seen him play a game of baseball.

By then I knew so much more about Darren than I had early in our relationship, most of it from talking with his mother, and that knowledge made it easier to make excuses for his brutish behavior. He had reasons to be angry. Darren said he came from a family with money. He said his mother was a nuclear engineer and his father showered him and his two brothers with gifts. His mother said he dreamed up that perfect childhood and probably started to believe it himself.

The truth, according to Verna, was that she and her kids lived in a trailer in Louisiana. Darren's parents divorced when he was six, around the same time he started sucking his thumb. His father was abusive, and his mother was not and had never been a nuclear engineer. Years after she divorced Darren's father, she remarried a construction worker, and her job was as a housewife raising three boys. The lies went on and on. No one had ever seen any evidence of Darren's college career, and if he did attend any school at all, his mother didn't know it. He had disappeared for a while after high school, she said, but neither she nor his brothers ever knew where he went. Verna said she didn't understand why he made up stories, but she'd never attempted to question him about it. Her habit had always been to look the other way rather than confront him about anything.

Darren was obviously ashamed of where he came from, so he embellished to impress others. He thought that to fit in with the crowd he wanted to fit in with, and that included me, he had to be something he wasn't. He had to be a big deal. So he developed the character he wished he was and tried to act the part. Being James Brown's son-in-law was part of that profile and one of the few things Darren told people that was true about his life. It was a big boost to his résumé and to his ego (and it was legitimate!) and he used it whenever he could. I heard him tell business associates, "When you hear of her dad passing away, just say *cah-ching!* She's going to be a very rich girl." I hated it when he said that, but I rationalized that it was just his way to get business, to show we weren't hurting financially so that investors were more likely to do business with him.

Darren's lying ways were bound to catch up with him. His deceptions were too big and too many for him to keep up the ruse forever. Unfortunately, a lot of people would end up hurt before the truth was revealed. Darren's investors would pay a big price for his deceit. Some invested their life savings in his shell games and lost everything.

We suffered, too.

20

Broke

"Lying to ourselves is more deeply ingrained than lying to others."
—Fyodor Dostoyevsky

I FIRST REALIZED we were broke when a process server showed up at our front door in Sugar Land in 2003. I know it's hard to believe that I, with my urbane background and advanced education, could have been so naive. I call it denial—deep denial. How could we have no money when Darren's business was solvent and I was working two pharmacy jobs and bringing in two salaries totaling $250,000 annually? I admit I didn't know exactly where my money was going. I presumed it was helping to pay our bills. I also had no idea that Darren's business was a sham. He had been using investors' money to buy fancy cars and other accoutrements of wealth, but he hadn't paid a mortgage payment for months. We were so far in arrears that the bank was threatening to foreclose on the house.

Darren owed thousands of dollars in back rent for his office space in Houston. Our pool company put a lien on our house for unpaid pool-cleaning bills. The veterinarian even returned a check for $241 he wrote that bounced. That was just the tip of the iceberg. Every day, I learned about someone else who was coming after us for unpaid bills. By the time I knew we were in trouble we were so far underwater, to the tune of close to a million dollars, there seemed little hope of recovering.

I asked Darren what the hell was happening. He said something about it being a bad year. It was a bad year? We were having a bad life, and it was about to get worse. I certainly didn't know then that for the three years we had been in Texas, he had been effectively using his investors' money to pay for our lavish lifestyle with spurious promises he knew he couldn't deliver on. To this day, I don't think Darren went into situations intending to steal from people. He really was smart and quite capable of making a good living. Many times he had brilliant ideas, and people did invest in them, but he didn't seem able to follow through. Unbeknownst to me, his cash flow had been drying up for months because people were catching on to him.

It may seem hard to believe, but I only really learned the extent of Darren's misdeeds four years ago when I read a story about him in *Atlanta* magazine. The reporter knew more about my husband's business dealings than I did. The story, called "The Debtor," explained Darren's transgressions anecdotally. It told of one instance involving our pastor in Texas, Dr. Steve Ams. Pastor Ams had been counseling Darren.

According to the magazine piece:

The men got to talking. Ams told Darren a story. A few months earlier, Ams had struck a deal with a mining company to trade precious metals from the Congo. But Ams had overplayed his hand. He had neither the technology nor the expertise to honor the agreement. He needed an international marketing strategy

and a computerized mineral-trading floor by the end of May
or the deal would collapse. What a coincidence. Darren was
chairman and chief executive of Lumar Worldwide Industries,
an international corporate-services company with more than a
hundred employees on three continents. Did he mention he was
an attorney licensed in California?

More lies, and to our own minister! Darren wasn't licensed as
an attorney in California or any other state, and his company had
fewer than a half-dozen employees, all of them located in Texas.

The magazine story went on to say that Darren drew up a contract for our pastor that was more indicative of a loan shark than
a legitimate businessman. For his services, Darren "required four
monthly payments of $35,000 and fourteen more monthly pay-
ments of $16,420. Late payments would draw interest of 10 percent
per day." Per day! Pastor Ams signed the contract; God knows why.
He paid Darren $140,000 over four months and got nothing in
return. I found myself wondering if our pastor's money paid for one
of the new cars in our driveway. Pastor Ams ended up taking Darren to court and winning a judgment against him for the money he
lost. Of course, Darren never paid.

When business was going badly, and it just kept getting
worse, the tension between Darren and me intensified. Bill col-
lectors closed in, making Darren more ornery than usual, and I
was always afraid of saying something that might set him off. It
was a losing battle, trying to avoid the inevitable punishment for
saying or doing something that rubbed him the wrong way. One
night, while we were having words about something, I don't even
remember what, he punched me so hard in the face that I saw stars
and nearly blacked out. I called the police and then did what I
always did: refused to sign a complaint when they came. Things
were bad enough without my husband being in jail, I reasoned. It

wasn't about just him and me anyway. We had the kids to think about. I had become an expert at kidding myself. As our life in Texas spiraled out of control, I decided that maybe all we needed was a change of scenery again. Darren was all for it. We filed for bankruptcy—I would learn it was Darren's third time filing—and his relatives moved us back to Georgia as the bank in Texas began foreclosure proceedings on our home.

Looking back, I am reminded of a passage from the book *But I Love Him* by Amanda Grace.

> But even when I stop crying, even when we fall asleep and I'm nestled in his arms, this will leave another scar. No one will see it. No one will know. But it will be there. And eventually all of the scars will have scars, and that's all I'll be—one big scar of a love gone wrong.

21

Trouble in Paradise

"Everything that irritates us about others can lead us to an understanding of ourselves."

—Carl Jung

WHILE I CONTINUED to do whatever it took to hide my marital woes, Dad and Tomi Rae seemed to enjoy exploiting theirs. Their bitter public spats always made it into the news. Finally, after less than two years of a tumultuous marriage, they announced their separation with a full-page ad in the show business trade paper *Variety*. The press had a field day with that one.

"The ad features a photo of the couple and their now two-year-old son, James Joseph Brown II, smiling at Walt Disney World while posing with the costumed character Goofy," the Associated Press wrote in a story that was picked up around the world.

Above the photo, a statement said that career demands had taken a toll on the marriage, but the split was amicable. *Variety* reported: "A colleague of Brown's said the photo was chosen to emphasize the happy times of the relationship, rather than the hard times of a breakup."

Was it all just a publicity stunt? I didn't think so at the time. In fact, I prayed it was true. For my father to be living with another addict was a recipe for disaster. I used to pray he'd find someone more stable. But in an interview with Larry King on CNN years later, Tomi Rae said the incident had indeed been for publicity.

"Well, we had an argument on an airplane," she told King. "And this happened many times. We had an argument on an airplane. And he wrote [the ad] on the airplane and called his secretary on the airplane and he told her to put it in [*Variety*]. He said it was great publicity and not to worry about it and to just—just to write it off.

"Now, we never broke up after that scene," Tomi Rae added. "We stayed together. That was our relationship."

I still don't know which version is true. Did they really break up? Or had it happened just as Tomi Rae said it did? I'm sorry to say that Tomi Rae has credibility problems, and my father never talked to us about his personal life, so there really isn't any way of knowing. What I do know is that theirs was like all of my father's relationships: volatile and violent. I was always waiting for that headline about him having smacked or pushed or punched her.

It came right after New Year's in 2004. One of Dad's confidants didn't like Tomi Rae and had been digging up dirt on her. He waited until he found something really juicy before presenting evidence to my father that his bride appeared to be nothing more than a gold-digging fraud. His investigation turned up evidence that Tomi Rae was already married to someone else, a Pakistani man, when she and my father had said their "I do's" at the house in Beech Island a couple of years earlier.

Dad, of course, hit the roof—and apparently Tomi Rae, too. *Rolling Stone* carried the story:

James Brown was arrested yesterday and charged with criminal domestic violence after he allegedly shoved his wife to the bedroom floor at their home in Beech Island, South Carolina.

The singer, 70, posted bond and was released on his own recognizance today. Thirty-four-year-old Tomi Rae Brown, Brown's fourth wife, was taken to the hospital and treated for scratches and bruises on her arm and an injury to her hip.

The press reported that the dustup began when the power went out in their house. It was cold outside and Tomi Rae wanted to check into a hotel until the power was restored. Dad refused.

I think what really happened is that Dad confronted Tomi Rae about being married to someone else. She admitted that she'd married a man named Javed Ahmed in Houston in 1997 but claimed she later learned that Ahmed was also married to three other women so a judge told her that her marriage to him was therefore not legal. Apparently Dad didn't believe Tomi Rae, and a shouting match escalated into a bedroom brawl. I had to wonder if PCP had found its way back into my father's life.

"Godfather of Soul Accused of Spouse Abuse—Again," read the headline in *Women's E-News* on February 1, 2004.

James Brown, the "Godfather of Soul," was back in jail on criminal domestic violence charges just two months after the prestigious John F. Kennedy Center for the Performing Arts in Washington, D.C., awarded Brown a lifetime achievement award. He received the honor despite the protests of women's rights advocates who claim that Brown's history of domestic violence and sexual harassment should have disqualified him for the award.

The fight didn't end with Dad shoving Tomi Rae. They were still carrying on a month later—this time not in the privacy of their home but on a commercial airline flight to a gig in Puerto Rico.

The *New York Daily News* reported that Tomi Rae was out of control on the flight, shouting at Dad and telling him, "I'm just here for damage control! You are in more trouble than you realize! So what if I was married to another man?" One passenger was quoted as saying, "She was causing a total scene, not trying to hide at all." Dad's publicist, Susan Blond, responded with "Mr. and Mrs. Brown are very much in love. Perhaps she said that in jest. She has a very dry sense of humor. They've reconciled, and the charges have been dropped."

She said it in jest? A dry sense of humor? I guess that's what publicists are paid for, covering up the truth when their clients mess up. At any rate, Tomi Rae told one reporter that Dad wasn't any more abusive than any other man. He didn't intentionally hurt her or anyone else for that matter, she said. His violence was a reflection of how he felt about himself. I suppose denial was the way Tomi Rae chose to be able to stay with my father. Who was I to criticize? I'd been covering up the truth about my bad marriage from the very first day. What became clear to me was that Tomi Rae equated abuse with love, and so did I.

My grandfather
"Pop," Dad, and
Mom, circa 1975.

Dad at the airport heading
out on tour, circa 1974.

Dad and Mom on their fifth
wedding anniversary, 1975.

Dad, Mom, and Deanna,
circa 1971.

Dad talking
business on the
phone while
having his hair set.

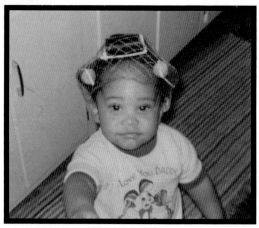

Me showing off curlers
just like Dad's.

Having fun in the pool at the Augusta, Georgia, home, circa 1974.

Ms. Ella Overton was a second mother to me.

Deanna and me, circa 1973.

My beloved pony, Sugar.

My mother's prized
Afghan, Fuzzy.

Me and Deanna, circa
1975.

Dad always went all out for Christmas, and our black Santa was a highlight of the display.

A family photo of Mom, Venisha, Deanna, and me, circa 1977.

Dad and I visited the Eiffel Tower
on a trip to Paris to celebrate my
twenty-first birthday.

Hanging out in our home
in Beech Island, South
Carolina, circa 1985.

Dad and Mr. Cannon
discussing business en route
in a private plane.

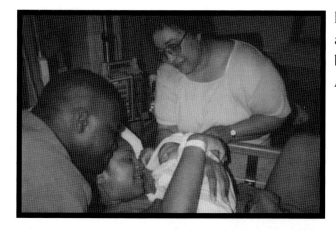

Darren, my mother, and I celebrate the birth of Sydney on April 15, 1999.

Sydney, Darren, and I pose for a holiday photo, circa 2000.

Sydney cuddles with her new baby brother, Carrington.

Sydney and Carrington showing off their Disney World souvenirs, 2009.

With my kids at an Atlanta Hawks game, December 2013.

22

Back to Atlanta

"Never give in, never give in, never, never never."

—*Winston Churchill*

I TALKED MYSELF into the idea that, after the Texas calamity, moving home was just what Darren and I needed. We would get a fresh start in Atlanta, surrounded by family and friends. We lived with my mom for a few months, but then I received an unexpected windfall that helped get us back on our feet.

My good fortune was well documented in the media—except they got the story all wrong. Deanna and I had settled a lawsuit we'd brought against Dad. Yes, you read it right. We sued our father for back royalties on songs we had contributed to as kids. The headlines were sensational and, needless to say, made my sister and me look like ungrateful, moneygrubbing scoundrels. What kind of children sue their parents?

In our case? Children who were following their father's advice. This is the real story of what happened: I had spoken with Dad right after he signed a bond deal for an advance on his music royalties. During that conversation, he told me something I didn't know. He said that he'd credited Mom, Deanna, and me as contributing writers on some of his songs, and that, once we turned eighteen, his record company should have been sending us royalty checks for our contributions. He said we should hire an attorney to look into it. So that's what we did. We took Dad's advice and hired an attorney, who eventually filed the lawsuit against the record company—but also named Dad because he had been receiving the royalties that legally belonged to us. Despite how the media played it, there was no family feud or grudge fest. Deanna and I did what our father suggested. We wouldn't even have known we were entitled to royalties if he hadn't told me about it. He was happy that we'd recouped the money that was legally ours. For me, it meant getting a chance at a new start.

With my royalty check in hand Darren and I went house hunting. We chose a house in the Atlanta suburb of Lithonia, a thirty-minute drive from the city, where many of the city's African American elite had settled. The house was substantial, with six bedrooms and seven baths and a price tag of well over a million dollars. I used my royalty check for the down payment, and we signed a lease-purchase contract in which we agreed to pay $10,000-plus per month until the house was officially ours.

Darren assured me we could afford to live in such luxury. If I could manage the rent for the first couple of months, he said, he would take over the payments once he got his new business off the ground. I had gotten a six-figure job at a pharmacy and figured I could carry us for a short time, so I agreed. I don't know what I was thinking. I wasn't even clearing $10,000 per month. I was living in La-La Land because I preferred that place to reality. But six months into our new beginning, the truth came calling in a way I couldn't ignore. After those first couple of months of me scraping together enough to pay our monthly bills, I couldn't keep up anymore. We were already too far behind on our house payments to catch up. We had to leave.

Darren had started a new venture capital company he called Pinnacle. He leased space in an opulent office building in downtown Atlanta and hired a staff. The perception around town was that my husband was a financial genius, but he wasn't bringing in any money. We explained to the owner of our house that we were having trouble and would have to break the lease. She didn't take out a judgment against us, but she did keep my deposit. We moved with the kids to an extended-stay hotel.

Shortly afterward, I filed for divorce. I was tired of Darren's lies and tired of him putting me down all the time. He didn't just degrade me in private anymore. He did it around the kids and with our friends. The late nights and philandering wore me down even more. And his thumb-sucking was driving me crazy. How had I been able to overlook it for so long? A grown man with his thumb stuck in his mouth. I begged him to suck on candy instead, but nothing seemed to work. He was addicted to sucking his damn thumb.

Darren talked me into seeking counseling through our church and, eighteen days after I filed, I withdrew the divorce complaint and we reconciled. The counseling seemed to help at first. His attitude changed and he was kinder to me. We both agreed to really work at the marriage. But after a while, everything went back to the way it had been. My solution was to numb myself and put any energy and love I had left into my kids.

Meanwhile, unbeknownst to me, Darren had been looking for a new place for us to live. He'd found just the place, he said. In fact, he'd been looking at it for a long time. The house was on a tony cul-de-sac called Tuxedo Court in Buckhead, the richest and most desirable section of Atlanta. I told Darren he was crazy. We couldn't afford Lithonia. How in the heck were we going to live in a zip code that was referred to as the Beverly Hills of the South? To give you a snapshot of Buckhead, the average income of its residents is in the mid six figures. Elton John has a place there. Sean "P. Diddy" Combs owns one of the local restaurants. The average price of a home is the high six figures (and that'll get you a townhouse). The one Darren had his heart set on was a monster house with a guesthouse and a pool and was assessed in the millions. I told him that after losing our house in Texas and then our house in Lithonia, I could not and would not have anything to do with a property I couldn't afford. Tuxedo Court was way out my league. Not to worry, Darren said. He would pay for it with money he was expecting from a business deal.

We moved to Tuxedo Court in February 2006. Darren negotiated the lease-purchase agreement. In it, he promised to pay the owners $25,000 per month in rent and $2.9 million cash by September. I didn't know then what the deal entailed. I didn't want to know, and I would learn about the crazy terms only much later, when it was too late to try to do anything about it. What in the devil was Darren thinking? We had already lost two houses of much lesser value because we couldn't pay the bills. Did he really think he could come up with nearly $3 million in seven months, on top of the enormous monthly rent? Either my husband was truly delusional or he had a boatload of cash I didn't know of. Of course he didn't.

The house was a spectacular 13,600 square feet of extravagance, with a two-story grand foyer, a designer kitchen with an island big enough to skate on, a home theater, a wine cellar, and fireplaces in half the rooms. I felt like a movie star every time I glided down the sweeping central staircase. Arthur Blank, a cofounder of The Home Depot and owner of the Atlanta Falcons football team, lived next door. My father was a superstar, but I'd never lived in a place like that. And, even though Dad could have afforded it, he never did either. We settled in quickly. Before long, we were throwing lavish parties for potential investors for Darren's new business. Darren said perception was everything, and the perception was that we had it all. The marriage was coming unraveled, but we looked like the perfect couple, with perfect children, living in the perfect house, on the perfect street, in a perfect zip code. Darren did whatever he could to perpetuate the myth. He told one person he was the thirty-first richest black man in the world (where he got that number, I'll never know) and another that he was the only black professional polo player in the United States. Obviously, nothing had changed.

I was thirty-three years old, had two beautiful kids, lived in a house worth millions, with a Range Rover and a Mercedes roadster in the driveway, and I was miserable. My husband was a fraud. My marriage was a sham. And we were living the life of the rich and famous when, in reality, we were neither. I continued to overlook things I shouldn't have—evidence of other women, bills piling up, escalating abuse, lies, lies, and more lies—but I desperately wanted to keep my family together. So I did whatever it took to not upset my husband, exactly what my mom had done with my dad, exactly the thing I promised myself way back when that I would never do.

That summer really put my marriage to the test. In July, on the heels of him being named a Goodwill Ambassador of the United Nations (sometimes connections pay off), Darren was accused of rape by one of his female employees. It was all over the news. "JAMES BROWN'S SON-IN-LAW CHARGED WITH RAPE." It was a nightmare. Darren called his mother and told her not to watch the news. He called my father to say he was sorry for tarnishing his name. He didn't apologize to me. When I asked about it he told me it was none of my business. I learned more from the news than I did from my husband. During a court hearing, according to TV reports, Jasmine Palmer said of Darren: "He'll make his advances toward me, grope me and touch on me, and I tried to not say anything and tried to just brush it off, but it was just getting overbearing. Then he got me cornered up in a room, basically, and forced himself on me." Darren was a no-show at the hearing.

After that, more women came forward and charged my husband with sexual misconduct at work. They said he wasn't just lecherous. He paid them with bad checks. One of the accuser's boyfriends called me and said she'd back off for the right price. They were basically trying to extort money from me. Women were coming out of the woodwork. Still, I stood by him. I didn't know what to believe. I suspected there was some truth to what the women were saying, but I didn't believe he was capable of rape. He eventually pleaded guilty to simple battery and misdemeanor sexual battery in exchange for probation and a few days in jail but only after eight months of pure hell for me.

Each new stress produced more strife in our marriage. Darren was drinking scotch every day, and he frequently accused me of infidelity. I learned that his business was, as it had been in Texas, based on deception and lies. He made deals with spurious promises and his investors' money disappeared. One investor lost his home. Another lost her life's savings. I don't know where the investors' money went. Darren kept anything to do with money hidden from me. I paid for the nanny and the housekeeper and other household bills and figured he was taking care of his financial responsibilities, which included the mortgage. I knew that Darren occasionally sold off stock to help pay our monthly bills, but he had begun selling stock every month, and his resources had all but dried up. I knew from experience what was next: sheriff's officers with eviction papers would be knocking at the door. Letters would arrive from lawyers representing Darren's business victims.

Darren slept fine at night, but I was sick with worry. My life was shattering around me, and I felt helpless to rescue myself. I lay awake wondering what else could possibly go wrong.

Then my father died.

23

A Family Divided

*"It's loss and regret and misery and yearning that drive
the story forward, along its twisted road."*
—*Margaret Atwood*, The Blind Assassin

TOMI RAE WAS in rehab in Malibu, California, when Dad died. She said she went for a prescription drug habit that developed after her father had died several months earlier. The way she tells it, Dad sent her away to get better because he felt somehow responsible for her habit. I have no reason to disbelieve her about that. She said she spoke with him just before the dental appointment that led to his hospitalization and didn't even know he was ill until Mr. Bobbit called early on Christmas morning. At the time, she was in a therapy session at rehab and didn't get the message until it was too late to get back from California in time to be with Dad. I felt bad for Tomi Rae. Dad's death was so unexpected and all of us had deep regrets about missing the chance to say goodbye. I'm sure she felt a lot of guilt over not being there with him when he passed, just as I did. The way she conducted herself afterward, however, made an almost unbearable time in all of our lives even harder.

We, my father's family, were dismayed to see the photos of Tomi Rae on her knees, gripping the wrought iron gate to the house in Beech Island. I understand how upsetting it must have been to come home to a padlocked gate and to have her own guards, the ones she'd hired, refuse her admittance to "Mr. Brown's house" unless she could produce a marriage license—which, of course, she didn't have with her. Who carries around her marriage license? (The guards later said they were instructed by Dad's lawyers to lock the gates to protect against looters.) What I objected to most was that she gave people the impression that we, Dad's children, were behind the lockout when, in fact, it was the trustees of the estate—three of Dad's business associates—who wouldn't let her in. And as far as her complaints about being photographed kneeling at the gate, well, the photographers were in place before she arrived. She saw them aiming their cameras at her, and then she got hysterical and fell to the ground.

Tomi Rae claimed we were monstrous to her after Dad died. Not only did we lock her out of her home, she said, we did everything we could to freeze her out of the funeral services. She even accused us of taking covert action to exclude her, giving her times and places to meet to go to each of the services and then leaving without her. None of it was true.

In retaliation for what she described as the total humiliation she suffered at the time, Tomi Rae did a series of interviews in the month after Dad's death with anyone who would listen to the crap she had to spew. The funny thing is, she aimed her anger more at Dad than us, attacking his dignity and, in the process, forever besmirching the image he'd worked his whole life to build.

I'll give you a good example. An "exclusive" with London's *Daily Mail* began this way:

Far from being a sex machine, [Brown] was a sick old man struggling to come to terms with his fading libido. He was tortured
by bouts of paranoia and was deeply insecure. And he subjected
those closest to him to violence and cruel threats of emotional
blackmail. . . . In her first interview since his death, [Tomi Rae
Hynie] shatters the myth of a soul legend.

This was the man she was supposed to love intensely and completely, and what does she do? She paints Dad as a pathetic figure,
a decrepit old man who was suffering from diabetes and crippling
arthritis. If that weren't degrading enough, she went on to say that,
far from his public persona as a "sex machine," Dad had a difficult
time making love, even with the aid of Viagra.

During the same week, she went on *Larry King Live* on CNN
and slammed everyone, including Deanna and me, claiming we had
treated her and her son with disrespect and insinuating that we
were finagling to control Dad's estate. The interview was salacious
and accusatory. I'm sure a lot of viewers tuned in. Tomi Rae hit all
the bases. We were money hungry. We didn't care about our dad.
She even used her child in her diatribe against us.

Tomi Rae then went on to accuse Rev. Sharpton of being especially hostile toward her. She gave, as an example, an exchange
they had during the public service in Augusta when Rev. Sharpton
asked Deanna and I to come onstage while Shirley Lewis, the president of Paine College, presented Dad with a posthumous doctorate
degree. We knew Dad would be thrilled to receive the degree, and
we proudly obliged Rev. Sharpton's invitation. Tomi Rae followed
us onstage, uninvited. It was an awkward moment for everyone,
even more so than earlier when she jumped onstage, knelt over
Dad, and sang a rocking rendition of the Sam & Dave song, "Hold

On! I'm A Comin','" a song she and Dad had sung together on his last tour. At the end of the song, she picked a rose from one of the nearby flower arrangements and tossed it dramatically into the casket.

Her version of the presentation of the doctorate, as told to King, was that she took it upon herself to join us onstage because our father would have wanted it that way. When Rev. Sharpton handed the award to us, he said, "As I sit and watch Tomi Rae cry behind me, I know that she would be happy knowing that Mr. Brown sees that his daughters get these doctorates." Then, she said, he turned around to her and said, "See, I recognized you." She responded, "You still aren't going to give me the dignity of calling me his wife." And he shot back, "You see, I tried to be nice to you and look what you did. Now I ain't going to be nice to you no more. That's it." She walked off stage and wasn't allowed to give her eulogy, she said.

Tomi Rae and Rev. Sharpton did have an exchange of words that day. I don't recall exactly what was said. Rev. Sharpton did say something that offended her but only after she made a nasty comment about not being properly respected as James Brown's wife. What she seemed to be forgetting was that she still had the burden of proving she was Dad's wife and, until she offered that proof, no one was obliged to treat her as such. Not only that, she was making a mockery of the service with her constant interference.

The words that hurt the most during that time weren't about Rev. Sharpton or us, though, but Tomi Rae's one-dimensional characterization of Dad as a "monster." She told the London tabloid that Dad treated everyone around him badly. "Violence was something I got used to," she said. "One moment he was loving, passionate and romantic, the next he was a monster. He was a control freak. People around him were frightened of him. . . . [Our] home always had to be spotless and I had to be in by sundown every night because he was so jealous and possessive."

There were grains of truth I recognized but no balance, no mention of the James Brown who could be charitable and loving and kind. The whole story was disgraceful. I could hardly believe she would stoop to such a level.

She later explained her thought process in the interview with Charles Thomson for Sawfnews. "I didn't know what to do," she said. "I was so completely in shock and out of my mind and upset and angry at him for allowing that to happen. I was in such shock that I did some things that I'm not proud of. I spoke about things in our personal life that I shouldn't have mentioned. I was so angry— it was not a time that I should have been speaking to the press."

It was too little and too late to undo the damage she had done.

24

Contesting the Will

"There is an African saying which is: 'Be careful when a naked person offers you a shirt.'"

—*Maya Angelou*

IT WAS DEANNA and I and four of our half siblings who decided to contest Dad's will. Our decision wasn't based on greed or bitterness over the fact that the bulk of his estate was earmarked for educational scholarships for underprivileged kids. Dad always said he wanted a large part of his estate to go to charity. Our decision to contest the will was because of our distrust of the businessmen he named as trustees of the estate.

The will was, for the most part, straightforward. In the most basic terms, six of his children were named, including Deanna and me, to receive his personal belongings—cars, clothes, jewelry, furniture, photographs, letters, and career memorabilia, those kinds of things. Half of the rest of his assets were to be put in an education trust, first to fund college for his grandchildren and then for scholarships for needy children from South Carolina and Georgia. The other half was set aside to fund the administration of his legacy.

Dad said many times that our share of his estate would come from administering his agenda. For instance, we would be paid for setting up and running the I Feel Good education charity and for creating the James Brown memorial museum at his home in Beech Island, which he envisioned to be similar to Elvis's Graceland in Memphis, and for continuing his annual holiday turkey giveaway. The way he arranged it was consistent with his conviction that no one should get anything for nothing. We were raised with the belief that you worked for what you got, so that part of the will was not surprising, nor did we object to doing our part to carry out his wishes. In fact, we looked forward to devoting our careers to keeping Dad's memory alive. There was just one glitch: the way the will was written opened an opportunity for the three trustees—David Cannon, Buddy Dallas, and Alford Bradley—to control the estate and benefit to the tune of millions of dollars before we ever had a chance to implement any of the programs Dad wanted.

A few days after his death, we met with the trustees at Deanna's house in Beech Island to discuss Dad's estate. Darren and Deanna's husband, Shawn, were also present. Cannon said he and the other trustees were interested in working with us to carry out Dad's wishes. We expressed our concerns about the way the will was written and said we knew our father wanted us to be involved in the administration of his estate. Their solution was to name Deanna as a fellow trustee and give me some innocuous title, a gesture that was nothing more than a veiled attempt to stay in our good graces. Deanna and I said we would think about their offer.

At a follow-up meeting the next day, Cannon proposed giving us 5 percent of the estate, or $5 million, which was based on its value of $100 million. We asked about our four half siblings named in the will. It would be our responsibility to share our take with them, Cannon said. Number one, there was no way we were going to cut our family members out of the process. Second, their proposal meant the trustees still had tens of millions of dollars at their disposal as well as control of the copyrights to his vast music catalog, with no accountability except to each other. We still weren't guaranteed a say in how Dad's money was spent. Cannon was effectively trying to cut us out of the process.

Dad wouldn't have wanted that. He'd told us numerous times that he wanted us involved in carrying out his legacy, and that's what we were looking for. My sister and I had a bad feeling about Cannon. But the red flags really went up when he mentioned that he was in a hurry to close deals and tie up loose ends with Dad's estate because he was moving to Honduras. He's the trustee, with power of attorney, and he's moving out of the country at the beginning of a process that would certainly take months, if not years, to complete? How was that going to work? Darren said what all of us were thinking. "He's trying to run," he said. "I don't like this."

The will was set to be read on January 11, 2007, a little more than two weeks after Dad died. Louis Levenson, the same attorney who had represented Darren on the rape charges a few months earlier, was our legal counsel. Levenson filed a petition with the court accusing the trustees of mismanaging Dad's estate and asking for an independent accounting of his assets. Everything went sour from there.

The trustees fought to keep information from us. They insisted that only they knew what James Brown wanted, and they claimed he specifically didn't want his children to benefit from his estate. We knew that wasn't true and that they were manipulating the situation so as not to lose control. Then they turned their sights on

Tomi Rae, attacking her at every turn, calling her a gold digger and a clinger-on and worse, because they knew it was only a matter of time before she came asking for her piece of the pie. I'm sure it was a diversion tactic to take the focus off of them.

As we waited for a court-ordered accounting of Dad's assets from the trustees, Tomi Rae filed her lawsuit. The will had been drawn up before she and Dad had their wedding ceremony at Beech Island and before Little Man was born, and neither one had been provided for. Tomi Rae wanted half of everything Dad owned, but she had two big hurdles to cross before her case could proceed. One was that she had to prove that she and Dad were legally married, which was doubtful. The second was the paternity of her son. The trustees said they wanted proof that Little Man was Dad's biological child. Dad had had a vasectomy years before and they didn't believe he had been capable of fathering another child.

Attorneys for the estate went back to court to request DNA from our father's body, should the need to prove the paternity of Little Man arise. To get what they needed, Dad's legs would have to be amputated for bone marrow samples. Tomi Rae sat by Dad's side and said she held his hand during the process. I thought that was morbid. I couldn't bear to be there.

Meanwhile, we began to suspect that the trustees had been playing fast and loose with Dad's money. My father was street smart, but these men were educated in accounting and the law, and he was no match for their business expertise. Would he have even known if one or all of them was stealing from him? Why were they so opposed to sharing an accounting of his assets unless there was something to hide? The estate was shedding truckloads of money in administrative and attorney fees. Creditors were lining up, and the trustees weren't paying the bills. The estate still owed Mr. Reid $70,000 for the funeral.

Tomi Rae claimed she'd had a conversation with Dad in the months before he died and that Dad had begun suspecting that the trustees were draining money from his accounts. According to her, one account was minus millions, and when he asked them about it, no one could give him an explanation. She said Dad was despondent because he believed that the men he trusted for so many years had deceived him, and he didn't have the proof or the know-how to do anything about it.

Had Dad known about all of the infighting over his will, he would have been turning over in his grave. Except that he didn't have a grave. Nearly three months after his death, he had yet to be buried because no one could agree about where his final resting place should be.

I couldn't sleep at night, thinking about him lying in the cold basement of the funeral home, all alone, long after he should have been laid to rest.

25

No Place for Dad

"A friend is one who has the same enemies as you."
—*Abraham Lincoln*

AS THE TRUSTEES waged a fierce campaign to discredit everyone who questioned the validity of Dad's estate, the frosty relationship between Tomi Rae and the rest of us thawed. We all realized that we had to work together for right to prevail. Our first priority was trying to come to an agreement about where he would be buried.

The news media checked in regularly for a burial date. Weeks had passed with no resolution. "Where was the body?" the reporters asked. "How is it being preserved? When will he finally be buried?" I began reading stories in the press about Dad's body being kept in a temperature-controlled room in his house in Beech Island. I have to laugh every time I think about how absurd that is. Who in their right mind would keep a body in the house for weeks on end? Those stories are still out there, so I'm going to set the record straight right here and right now: Dad never returned home after his trip to the emergency room, alive or dead.

Mr. Reid, the funeral director, was Dad's keeper from the time his body was taken from the hospital to his ultimate burial in March 2007. The funeral home has a prep area that is kept cold for the corpses. People should have been able to read between the lines when Mr. Reid said in an interview that ran around the world that Dad's body was being held in a confidential location but that he personally checked on him regularly. "I do that constantly," Mr. Reid was quoted as saying in a story from the Associated Press. I guess it made a better story to say Dad was dead at home while his battling family couldn't agree on where to bury him. The truth was less sensational and more complicated.

Mr. Reid understood that we wanted to make the right decision about where Dad was buried. He told us not to worry about the body. Sometimes bodies were held in the funeral parlor for two or three weeks before they were finally buried. We had exceeded that by a couple of months already.

Because Tomi Rae still needed to prove she was legally married to Dad, Deanna and I had guardianship of his body. Our father had once said he wished to be buried with Adrienne and his father in Walker Memorial Park in Augusta. Later, he changed his mind to his Beech Island property. We wanted to bury Dad on his property, but it was tied up in our legal proceedings with the trustees, and we feared that as soon as the burial was over they'd be at the gate selling tickets to the public. To bury him next to Adrienne and Pop in that tiny public cemetery in Augusta didn't make sense, either. People would be traipsing all over the grounds to take pictures of James Brown's grave. The decision about what to do was time-consuming. Finally, in mid-February, we decided that the best place for Dad was on Deanna's property in Beech Island. It was private there, and he could rest in peace. If, after all of the legal rulings were made, we were able to carry out his wish that his home be turned into a memorial museum, we could transfer his remains there at a later date.

We consulted Tomi Rae, and she agreed that Deanna's house was the best option, so we set a date for the service. Only close friends and family were invited. We asked that they keep the date and place confidential to keep the paparazzi away. When the trustees learned about our plans, they were furious and took their gripe to the press. They had made arrangements for "a very prominent memorial garden" in Augusta, they said, a place that was befitting of someone of Dad's stature. How dare we bury the Godfather of Soul in someone's backyard?

26

The End of the Marriage

"And now you are and I am now and we're a mystery/
which will never happen again."

—E. E. Cummings

THE DAY I knew my marriage was over was Thursday, March 7, 2007, two days before Dad was to be buried on my sister's property in Beech Island. I know the exact date because it's on the arrest report. The legal wrangling over the estate was in full tilt, and I had just returned from a meeting with our lawyers. Darren had an office in our guesthouse, and I joined him there for a drink. He was sitting with my nephew, my half brother Terry's son, Forlando, and had already had his share of scotch. I could tell from his cocky stance and the drained Chivas bottle on his desk. Forlando's visits with Darren had become frequent after Dad died. I often told my nephew not to count on getting rich off of Dad, but Darren filled his head with other ideas. Ideas about how Darren could turn Dad's considerable wealth into so much more that everyone in the family would benefit from, if only we would turn over the reins to him.

That's all he'd talked about since Dad died. The estate. He wanted to manage it for the family. He could turn Dad's millions into billions with the right investments. That was his expertise. Would I *please* get my damn family to agree?

I poured myself a glass of red wine, sat down on the couch, and kicked off my heels. My feet hurt and I was bone tired, the kind of unpleasant tired that comes from stress.

"How was the meeting?" Darren asked. Right away, I could tell he was in a nasty mood.

"It was OK," I said, my voice hoarse with weariness. *Please don't start.*

Darren drummed his fingers on his desk. I was dreading the next question, but I knew it was coming. "Did you talk to your sister?" *Oh shit. I don't know if I can play the game right now. I'm not sure I have the stamina to try to keep the peace.*

A couple weeks earlier, at a meeting with me, my sister, and Rev. Al Sharpton, Darren had presented us with his business strategy for investing Dad's holdings. The man knew how to make a presentation. I'll give him that. He had made a career of bullshitting people into investing their money with him. He had been impressive that day with us, too, dressed in his best pin-striped business suit, talking about real estate and hedge funds and venture capital, that kind of stuff. When he finished his pitch, he asked Deanna and me to sign a contract, which basically gave him carte blanche to do as he pleased with our inheritance. No way was Deanna going for that, so the meeting ended without any kind of commitment. Darren had been stewing ever since.

My sister was especially leery of the part of Darren's plan that put him in charge of the estate. When I told him that afterward, he blew a gasket. "That stinking, rotten bitch!" he raged. "Who does she think she is?" He badgered me to pressure Deanna to see things his way, but even though I was too afraid to come right out and tell him, I wasn't about to try to talk Deanna into anything, nor could I. Deanna is a strong woman, and she didn't trust Darren, with good reason. She knew his history. He had blown his share of business deals—and our new house was on the way to foreclosure, for God's sake. Why *would* she put her future in his hands?

I hadn't raised the subject with Deanna again. We had too many other things on our mind. But Darren didn't like it when he didn't get his way. He wanted to manage Dad's holdings, and he wanted me to convince everyone involved—starting with my sister—that it was a good and sound financial decision to hire him. Time was a wastin'.

"Well?" he asked again, pouring himself another scotch and sneering at me. "Did you talk to Queen Bitch or didn't you?"

"Um . . ." I said. My shoulders tightened up, the way they always did when I felt a confrontation with Darren coming. I fumbled for more words, but they stuck in my throat.

"Um?" my husband asked, mocking me. "You said 'um'? Um what?" He picked up the half-smoked cigar that was smoldering in an ashtray on his desk. I looked into my wine glass and wished I were someplace else. Honestly, I wanted to haul off and punch him.

As I stood there, swirling the wine in my glass, he blew smoke rings and waited for an answer. "Well?" he asked. "Did you talk to her? DO YOU UNDERSTAND ENGLISH? DID YOU TALK TO HER?"

I sipped my wine and tried to explain. "It's not a good time, Darren," I said. "We're still mourning our Dad. We haven't even buried him yet. We can talk about the estate later."

I thought he might burst a vein in his head. He clenched his teeth, rolled his eyes, and shook his head from side to side. He didn't want to hear it. Who cared that my poor father had been kept in a crypt in a temperature-controlled room for the last three months while everyone fought over where he should be buried? Who gave a damn that my heart literally ached when I thought about never hearing Dad's wonderful, raspy voice again? Not my husband. Oh, no. Darren wanted to talk business. My family's business. He wanted to make his name on my dead father's back.

Darren stubbed out the cigar and got up from behind his desk. "Time's a wastin', Yamma," he said, menacingly, as he paced around the room. "You need to stand up to your family. I'm a businessman. I know how to do this. Don't be stupid. You have to convince your sister let me handle this, or you're going to end up with no money. Do you hear me?"

I looked down at my drink to avert his stare. The wine jiggled in unison with my shaking hand. I didn't want him to see that I was nervous, so I set the glass on the table. But my leg gave me away, jackhammering the way it always does when I'm anxious. Darren looked at my quivering leg and smirked. He loved being in control.

He began rambling on about my sister and me and how we thought we were so goddamn smart and knew so much when we didn't know shit from Shinola. I knew what would happen if I mouthed off so I held my tongue, but my silence only seemed to provoke him this time. He bent down and got in my face. His breath stank of cigar tobacco and booze.

"Areyoulisteningtome,Yamma?" he asked, his words jamming into each other. "Whathehell'swrongwithyou? . . . Doyouknow-howimportantthisis?"

I clenched my fists so tight my fingernails gouged the skin of my palms. I tried tuning him out, but his words got louder and meaner. "You and your fucking sister," he shouted. "What do you know about anything? You'll listen to me if you know what's good for you, and you'll get your goddamn sister to . . ."

The pressure in my head was so intense I felt as though my eyes might pop. I thought of all the things I wanted to scream at him about—years' worth of things I had stuffed inside to keep the peace. I was bursting with contemptuous thoughts. *Stop your carrying on, you damn lunatic. What makes you think you know anything? You're a liar and a loser. You're a grown man and you still suck your damn thumb, for God's sake!*

"I'm not going to try to convince my sister to do anything, Darren," I said firmly, interrupting my husband in the middle of his rant. "Please! Just let me mourn my dad." He stopped shouting and stared at me. He was stunned that I was talking back. How dare I? "Besides," I continued, picking up my wine glass and standing to leave, "it seems as if this is about giving control of the estate over to you, and I'm not comfortable with that." *Wrong answer, Yamma.*

Darren lurched at me, cursing and spewing his rage with such force that his spit sprayed my face. "Who do you think you are?" he shouted. "You stupid bitch. You and your family don't know what you're doing. You're going to fuck up everything." I wiped his saliva from my cheeks and turned to walk away. "Do you hear me?" he yelled, his voice seething with scorn. "You have no idea how to run this, and neither does anyone else in your family. What the hell do you know about anything?" God, I hated him. "Don't you walk away from me! Don't you *dare* walk away."

"You're crazy!" I cried. "You need help!"

My nephew leapt from his chair and tried to intervene. "C'mon, Uncle Darren," he pleaded. "Just try to calm down." Darren pushed Forlando to the side then grabbed my arm. I yanked it away. He pushed me, and I shoved my hand in his chest and pushed him back. Now mind you, I am five foot one and 110 pounds compared to his six foot five and 280 pounds. "I'm not dealing with this tonight," I said. "I don't want to talk about the estate. You're right, Darren. I don't know anything." He pushed me harder. The wine glass flew out of my hand and shattered on the floor.

I don't know what came over me, but I wasn't going to let this man have the upper hand. Not this night. And not the next. Or the night after that. I was done. I could feel it in my soul. My father was dead, and as much as I always wanted him to somehow save me, now he truly never would. If I were going to get out of this marriage alive, I would have to save myself. And I was ready.

"Don't put your fucking hands on me," I said. "I'm not in the mood for your shit." *Now you've done it, Yamma.*

Darren's eyes bulged out of his head. Sweat poured down his face. "You said *what?*" he asked, incredulous.

"I said I'm not in the mood for your shit," I repeated, holding my ground.

My defiance only fueled his rage. He shoved me and I hit the wall with a loud thud. I gathered myself and walked toward the door, hoping he'd let me go. He followed on my heels, cursing me. "You ungrateful, stupid, fucking bitch!" he shouted. I could feel his hot breath on my neck.

I walked into the main house and headed for our bedroom. My plan was to get far enough ahead of Darren to lock myself inside. I ran through the living room and he pushed me from behind. I stumbled over the cherry curio cabinet in the hallway and heard the china inside rattle. "Leave me alone, you son of a bitch," I screamed.

We reached the bedroom and I tried to shut him out, but he knocked me to the floor before I could get the door closed. I twisted my knee and watched helplessly as he stomped over to my closet and tore all my clothes from their hangers and threw them in heaps on the floor. "Stop it!" I screamed. "Stop it!" I crawled toward the open bedroom door. Darren grabbed my leg and I kicked him off. *Someone's going to die,* I told myself. *I have to live for my kids. I have to get out of here.*

Struggling to my feet, I stumbled out of the bedroom and down the hallway. I was screaming in fear, but there was no one else there and Darren was in hot pursuit. He grabbed me from behind and heaved me toward the kitchen. I lost my balance. *This is it,* I thought. *I'm going to die.*

I know it's a cliché, about seeing your life flash before your eyes, but I really did. As I tried to keep from falling, I saw myself as a little girl, dressed in my yellow sundress, wandering away to see my pony, Sugar. I saw myself, a few years later, pounding on my father's back and begging him to stop pummeling my mother. I saw my father walking me down the aisle at my wedding and I remembered the moment, just before we reached the altar, when I wished he would rescue me from making the biggest mistake of my life. But my father never rescued me, not even when I told him years earlier that Darren beat me. Why did I think he could? No one ever rescued my mother or stopped my father from beating her. I wondered if he even understood that beating a woman was wrong.

Backing into the kitchen, I saw the paring knife on the counter. I grabbed it and started swinging. Darren's eyes said everything. I knew that at that moment he could kill me. "Leave me alone!" I cried. Darren lunged at me. We scuffled for a few seconds. I stuck the knife in his forearm and watched as blood trickled onto the floor. I tried to run away, but he grabbed me from behind, spun me around, and drove his fist into my face. I went down, and my head smacked the tile floor. Warm blood seeped from a gash in my scalp. I imagined gooey yoke oozing from a cracked egg.

I lay there for a moment, trying to focus, wondering how badly my head was bleeding, questioning whether I would even be able to save myself. If I could keep from losing consciousness, I still had a chance. *My kids,* I thought. *I have to win this battle for my kids.* My nephew appeared and tried to pick me up, but I screamed out in pain. I could barely move my mouth. It hurt to try to talk. I heard Darren rummaging through my closest, pulling all of my clothes off the hangers. I lay very still as he paced back and forth between our bedroom and the kitchen. Had he lost his mind?

"You cut me!" he screamed. "You fucked up. You're going to jail and I'm going to get the kids. Now get your sorry ass up."

At that moment, lying on that cold tile floor, with my head pounding and my vision blurred, I saw my marriage with absolute clarity, and I knew it was over. I'm not sure why I was so certain this time. Maybe Darren had finally beaten the pretense out of me. My marriage had survived for ten years on false hope and make-believe. Now there was nothing left but the bare and brutal truth. I was an abused woman and I wasn't going to take it anymore. Any feelings I still had for Darren were finally dead. Now if only God would let me live. That's when the room went black.

When I woke up, I was alone in my kitchen. I was astonished and furious that my own nephew had abandoned me while I lay unconscious on my kitchen floor, without knowing if I would live or die. The house was eerily quiet. I picked myself up off the floor and dragged my aching body from room to room to make sure Darren wasn't lurking around a corner somewhere. When I knew I was safe, I called my sister first and then my best friend, and they both urged me to call the police, which I did. Then I called my mom. "What happened?" she asked. "I'm hurt, Mom," I said. "I need to get to the hospital." Mom arrived before the police. She knew that Darren was verbally abusive, but she didn't know about the previous beatings I'd taken. She looked me over and shook her head. I had never seen her look so sad. She didn't say a word. She didn't need to. We drove to the hospital in silence.

I winced as an emergency room nurse wiped the gash on my head. "Any dizziness?" she asked. "A little," I said. "Do you have any pain?" *Funny question*, I thought. I'd been in pain for most of my marriage. Now, other than the sting of the saline on my cuts and a throbbing headache from hitting my head on the floor, I just felt numb. "I'm OK," I answered. "The doctor will be by in a minute," the nurse said, pushing open the curtain around my bed and walking away.

My mother sat on the edge of my bed. "I hope this is the last time, Yamma," she said.

I stared at the hospital monitor over my head. My blood pressure and my heart rate belied my composure.

"Not now, Mom," I said.

She pressed on. "You don't have to put up with this."

I didn't want to hear that from my mother. In a way, I blamed her for what was happening to me. Hadn't she set the example? "You put up with it," I said. I was sorry as soon as the words left my mouth.

"I didn't have a doctorate, Yamma," my mother said. "You can pick up the pieces."

Yes, I thought. *I can pick up the pieces.* I won't live in a multimillion-dollar Greek revival mansion in Buckhead anymore and I won't drive a big, bad Range Rover, but having those things was never my dream; it was Darren's. I knew all about material things. The biggest house in Beech Island didn't make my father feel good enough about himself to stop threatening my mother, and the Mercedes in the garage didn't comfort my mother after she took a beating from him. The only "thing" I ever really wanted was a happy home and to know real love. I had fooled myself into thinking that I could have that with Darren. I couldn't kid myself any longer.

The doctor had just finished checking me over when the police arrived at my bedside. My nose was broken and I couldn't open my mouth without it hurting like hell. Bumps and bruises covered my arms and legs. Darren was at the other end of the emergency room, one of the officers said. He was getting stitches for the stab wound. He wanted me arrested. "He said you did it. Is that true?" "Yes," I said. "Well, sort of. He was beating me. I thought he was going to kill me. I grabbed the knife to defend myself. He tried to get it away. He got stabbed." Darren told the cops that I was trying to get rid of him and had tried to stab him in the heart. "We have to charge you with aggravated assault," the other officer said, almost reluctantly. "Me?" I cried. "Me?" I couldn't believe what I was hearing. "He was going to kill me. All I did was try to save my own life."

My mother wailed. "Please, officers," she pleaded. "Don't take my daughter away tonight. You don't understand. There's a long history of abuse here. And in two days this girl is burying her father."

This is really bad, I thought as I sat there, watching my poor mother beg for me. How had this happened? How had I become the woman I vowed never to be? I looked from the officers, into my mother's weary eyes, and, for the first time in my life, I could see past the image of who I had wanted my father to be, to the truth of who he really was—a deeply flawed man who had been incapable of restraining his own violence, much less saving me. And Darren? I was in love with the idea of Darren, not the person he was—the same way I loved the idea of having a perfect father. How can you love someone who hurts you so much?

My mother took me home with her that night. Deanna had picked up my kids at their friend's house and brought them to Mom's. "What happened to you?" they cried when I walked through the door. "Mommy had an accident," I said. "Don't worry. I'm fine."

"Where's Daddy?" Sydney asked.

"Daddy's home," I said. "We're going to stay with grandma tonight. Now let's all go to sleep."

Of course, I didn't sleep.

I brought a police officer with me when I went back for my clothes the next day. Darren was still in a fighting mood. "You'll have to kill me first," he said when the officer told him why we were there. He took a step toward us. The officer pulled out his pepper spray and aimed it at him. Darren threw up his hands and backed away. "Sorry, man," he said. "This has been a stressful time." The officer ordered Darren to wait outside while I retrieved what I needed from the house. I never looked at Darren, but I could feel his eyes burning into me. After I left, he sent me a text message. "I will do everything in my power to see you put away for 10 years," it said. He later told an Atlanta newspaper that he had thought we were happily married, "But I guess she wanted out, and she figured by killing me she gets out." Poor Darren, always the victim. *Go suck your thumb*, I thought.

That Saturday morning I sat at my father's graveside on my sister's property in Beech Island, wearing big sunglasses to hide my black eyes and a long-sleeved blouse to cover my bruises. My dress was white, a symbol of the celebration of my father's life. The day was glorious, with a gentle breeze blowing. I sat between my mother and my sister. Darren showed up, but security guards, at my instruction, turned him away. Rev. Sharpton spoke for a few minutes about Dad's accomplishments. I felt both proud and confused. The crypt was unveiled, and I imagined Dad's spirit floating up to the brilliant blue sky. I prayed for his soul. I prayed for us all. When the service was over, I dropped a rose at the foot of the crypt and walked with my mother to our waiting car. The police had given me the time to say my goodbye to my dad. Now it was time to turn myself in.

As we drove away from my sister's, I saw Darren talking with the reporters who had gathered outside the gate. I read in the next day's papers that he was ranting about not being allowed to attend the burial. Darren couldn't see me through the dark, tinted windows of the limousine, but I saw him as clearly as if I were looking through a magnifying glass. I squeezed my mother's hand. The car drove on.

That afternoon, we drove to the police station and I turned myself in. I was charged with aggravated assault, a felony. My mug shot got blasted all over the TV. Just like Dad, I thought. I'd never imagined myself an accused felon. I had always been a pretty mild-mannered person.

The charges against me were dropped when Darren didn't show up for the court hearing. God is good. The following month, on April 4, 2007, I filed for divorce. Darren wasn't happy. He had lost his one legitimate claim to fame, that he was related by marriage to Mr. James Brown himself.

What bothered me more than anything was how involved our children had been in our troubles. My kids had seen the abuse I suffered. Carrington used to rub my nose every day after Darren broke it and tell me, "Mom, I'm sorry about your nose." Still, they loved their father, and, like most kids, they wanted us to be together as a family again, just as I had when we left Dad. Darren told the kids I was to blame. I was the bad guy. It was me who broke up our family, not him. He wanted our family back together again. I told the kids not to get caught up in our stuff. "Love your mom and love your dad; that's all you need to do," I said. Looking at their sad little faces, my heart broke into pieces, but I knew that in the long run they were better off with us apart.

I did all I could to avoid any face time with Darren, so he bombarded me with text messages every day, as was his habit when he was mad and couldn't confront me directly. Some of his messages were belittling. "Look at my suit! Where in the fuck did you learn to iron, you good for ABSOLUTELY NOTHING?" Some were for the kids. To Sydney, who was loyal to us both but closer to me, he wrote: "You are too young to know better, but you know that mommy cut daddy with a knife and I had 12 stitches in my arm?" Some were downright threats. "I'm going to expose you for the phony you really are. I'm setting up interviews with any network that will listen. I know your father was murdered." Murdered? Dear Lord. He really was nuts.

True to his word, Darren began talking to reporters and called for a full investigation of Dad's death. The insinuation was that my father was murdered and that I was somehow involved. It was an empty rant by a diluted, bitter man. Nevertheless, the negative publicity got me fired from my job.

27

Protecting Dad's Will

"A body of men, holding themselves accountable to nobody,
ought not to be trusted by anybody."

—*Thomas Paine*

THE SAME MONTH that I filed for divorce, a judge agreed with our family's request for a third party to oversee the trustees of Dad's estate. The job of the new administrator would be to "protect the estate by permitting all claims to be pursued and investigated with the required due diligence and will assist this Court in assessing the proper administration of the estate," Judge Jack Early said in his ruling. It didn't take long for the experts to find irregularities in the accounting.

That August, the court filed an order mandating that David Cannon be expelled from anything to do with Dad's estate, trusts, and "all Brown entities." The other two trustees, Mr. Dallas and Mr. Bradley, quit their posts begrudgingly but accused the judge of bullying them into the decision. For us, it was a victory. Judge Early then assigned two South Carolina attorneys as the new trustees. We were beside ourselves with joy.

In October, Cannon was ordered to pay back $373,000 of misappropriated funds from a $900,000 royalty check of Dad's as well as $50,000 in attorney expenses for our lawyers. If he didn't pay back the money, he would go to jail, the judge said. The royalty check was supposed to have gone toward a loan Dad took in 1999 against his future royalties, but Cannon said Dad had pocketed it instead and given him the cash he was now charged with taking illegally. Cannon told the judge he didn't have the money to pay back the estate. But he'd recently paid a contractor in Honduras more than a million dollars to build a home there, so the judge wasn't having any of his excuses.

We suspected that the royalty check was just the tip of the iceberg and that Cannon had mishandled millions of dollars that belonged to Dad. Nevertheless, we finally had the proof we needed that at least one of Dad's trustees could hardly be trusted to represent his wishes.

Cannon would later enter an Alford plea to two counts of breach of trust and be sentenced to three years of house arrest. The plea is not an admission of guilt but an acknowledgement that there was enough evidence against him for a conviction if he had gone to trial.

Ultimately, it took the firing of the court-appointed trustees and the intervention of a state attorney general to strike a settlement that seemed fair to everyone (except the former trustees). Under the deal brokered by South Carolina attorney general Henry McMaster and approved by Judge Early, 50 percent of Dad's estate would still fund the education trust for his grandchildren and college scholarships for needy students in South Carolina and Georgia. Tomi Rae would be entitled to 25 percent of the remaining assets, and Dad's children would benefit from the last 25 percent. Deanna and I and our siblings agreed that Tomi Rae did not have to prove that her marriage to Dad was legal. We knew he would have wanted her and Little Man to benefit from his estate. That was enough proof for us.

I wish I could say the deal was signed, sealed, and delivered, but the South Carolina Supreme Court overturned it in 2013 and, as of this writing, not a penny has been paid to anyone, including the needy kids Dad wanted to help.

28

A Shooting

"Every man's life ends the same way, and it is only the details of how he lived and how he died that distinguish one man from another."

—Ernest Hemingway

MY DIVORCE WAS final in October 2007, six months after I filed the papers with the court. Darren challenged me for custody of the kids, but I prevailed, thank God. The three of us moved in with my mom until I could get back on my feet. I quickly got another job in a pharmacy and earned enough that we could finally get our own place in the city. Darren had been evicted from Tuxedo Court and moved to a high-end townhouse community in Buckhead. He bought a new Mercedes and told friends he was earning upward of $500,000 a year. If that was true, we didn't see a penny of it. Knowing him the way I did, I was pretty sure it was all bravado.

I'm not sure how, but Darren and I eventually managed to forge a civil relationship. My reason for keeping him in my life was the kids. It gave them comfort to see that their father and I could still get along. Maybe it was easy for me because I truly didn't love Darren anymore. I didn't feel anything for him. I was glad to hear the news that he had a new girlfriend and relieved (and sorry for her) that his focus had moved to her.

We had been divorced for nearly a year when Darren proposed that we form a united front and travel with our kids to New York City to see our nine-year-old daughter, Sydney, perform a song from *The Lion King* at Carnegie Hall with her class from the Atlanta School of Performing Arts. I knew it would mean the world to Syd to have us there together for such an important event in her life, so I agreed. As the time for the trip grew closer, Darren began hinting that maybe the time together would be the beginning of reconciliation for us. I humored him, knowing that an outright rejection would ruin the trip for the kids, but I had no intention of going back to him. Not a chance. Not on your life. I was finally free from his grip and happier than I had been in years.

Two days before we were scheduled to fly to New York, Darren came to my job at the CVS Pharmacy to drop off the plane tickets because, he said, he was worried he might lose them. It was around 9:30 PM when he arrived at the pharmacy, and my shift was ending at 10:00. He had just picked up Sydney from her rehearsal at the Atlanta School of Performing Arts and dropped her off at my mom's, where the kids were staying for the night.

The date was November 5, 2008. President Barack Obama had just been elected the day before, and we talked about how we wished my Dad were alive to see the first African American president take office. He would have been so proud. While we were talking, Darren mentioned that he was headed back to his place to prepare a late-night dinner. I teased him about having a date, but he insisted it was a business dinner. We were both in good spirits, and he was smiling when he left. I watched through the window as his gleaming silver Mercedes pulled out of the parking lot and drove away. That was the last conversation we ever had.

Later that night, the wife of Darren's friend Chris called me at home. She sounded upset. When I asked what was wrong, she said, "Yamma, Chris just got a call from someone at Northside Hospital. They said Darren was shot. They said he's in bad shape and he is asking for you." I could barely breathe. Darren shot? I jumped in my car and raced to the hospital. All I could think about was my kids. As terrible as Darren had been to me, he was always devoted to his children, and they were to him. And I knew firsthand how difficult it was to lose a parent.

When I got to the emergency room, Darren was on life support. He didn't look like Darren. He looked gray and old and so sick. I knew he wasn't going to make it. His injuries were too severe. But I also didn't really comprehend at that point that he was going to die. I stayed in Darren's hospital room for the rest of the night, sitting by his bedside, watching as a machine pumped air into his lungs. It was hard, listening to the steady, mechanical whir of the machine but harder seeing Darren's distorted, swollen face.

When morning came, I ran home to get a shower, thinking I'd return to the hospital before I went to my job and again after work. But when I got back to his room, just a couple hours after I left, Darren was gone. I simply felt numb. I felt sorry for him and heartbroken for our children, who adored their father. And I was frightened for all of us. *Who did this?* I wondered. *And why?*

The police said Darren was ambushed as he drove into his gated townhouse complex. Darren pulled into his garage, and the gunman fired off three shots. Neighbors said they saw a black man wearing a hoodie running away, then Darren's Mercedes back out of the garage and head for the gate. The witnesses said that, as Darren waited for the gate to swing open, his car rolled back and struck a cement column. I figured he must have been losing consciousness at that point. They said the car then lurched suddenly forward, through the open gate, and sped off.

Lord knows how he did it, but Darren, mortally wounded, drove five miles to the hospital. Before losing consciousness, he made a request of the hospital staff: "Call my wife," he said. "I've got to live for my wife and kids." I have to say I was stunned that he was thinking about me when he was dying. We were long over and I never really believed him when he talked about wanting to get back together. Yet he'd called me his wife.

I sobbed when I looked at Darren in his casket. My tears were more about a child losing a parent. I had lost my dad only two years earlier, and I hurt for my kids. My own heartache was more about my memories and not the kind of grief you'd feel over losing a spouse. Darren and I were divorced, and no matter what he had said or done, he was not and would never have been, anything more to me again than my children's father. My love for him had withered and died long ago, but I had spent ten years of my life with the man and all of that time hadn't been bad. That's where the tears came from. There were good times, and those are what people tend to think about after someone is gone. I was no exception.

I wasn't just sad. I was also very afraid. People were theorizing that Darren had been the target of a hit. That didn't surprise me. He was always involved in shady things. I wondered what he had been involved in that would have cost him his life. What had he done to make someone want to kill him? Was it someone he'd burned in a business deal? If so, the list of suspects would be very long. There were countless cases that I knew of—of him taking someone's life savings, promising to turn it into millions, and when it didn't happen, not being able to explain where the initial investment went. So many people were pissed off at Darren. He'd made a lot of enemies. I suspected he'd finally betrayed the wrong person and the shooting was an act of revenge. But had that settled the score? At night I lay awake, listening to my heart pound in my chest, wondering if someone was going to break into our home, kidnap my kids, or kill us all.

And while I was busy looking over my shoulder for Darren's killer, the police were looking at me.

29

A Suspect

"A clear and innocent conscience fears nothing."
—*Elizabeth I*

I KNOW THE spouse is always a suspect when a husband or wife is murdered. And with my marital history and proof of our violent relationship documented in police reports from Georgia to Texas and back again, I had no doubt that the police were going to come looking for me. Waiting for the knock on the door was nerve-racking, even though I had nothing to hide. I couldn't imagine what it would be like for someone who did. Darren had been dead a few days when his landlord called to tell me that two detectives from the Atlanta PD were poking around the Buckhead townhouse. I decided that rather than waiting any longer for them to come to me, I would go to them.

The detectives were outside Darren's place when I drove into the driveway. With their broad shoulders, tight-fitting business suits, and military-style buzz cuts, they looked right out of central casting. "Hi," I said, walking up to them with my hand extended.

"I'm Yamma Brown Lumar, Darren's ex-wife." Their eyes widened and one tilted his head. "Ah!" he said. "We were planning to catch up with you, so it's really convenient you're here." I nodded, but I could feel my palms dampen. I'd never been involved in a murder investigation before and I didn't know what to expect. I'd seen my share of crime shows, where the cops play cat and mouse with their prey, trying to get them to trip up. I was determined to be completely candid with the detectives. Why wouldn't I be? "I'll help in any way I can," I said.

The detectives invited me into Darren's condo to talk. It was pretty messy and looked as if Darren would be returning home any minute. I saw food on the kitchen counter and clothes in a laundry basket on the floor, waiting to be washed. I noticed a photograph of a woman and assumed it was the girlfriend the kids had mentioned. But as I looked around, I saw snapshots of other girls scattered around and realized that Darren had been up to his old tricks. He was incapable of monogamy. He hadn't had *a* girlfriend. He'd had several of them. I wasn't surprised. The strangest and most inappropriate thought popped into my head. *I wonder if he sucks his thumb in front of them?* Then, just as quickly, *Stop it, Yamma!*

I took a seat in Darren's dark leather chair and the detectives sat on the couch across from me. They wasted no time. Taking turns, they pelted me with questions.

"Did Darren have a girlfriend?"

I glanced around at the photos. "I don't know, but my kids said he might have," I said.

"Were you upset about that?"

"Absolutely not," I answered honestly.

"Were you still seeing each other?"

"Not in that way," I said. "We were amicable for the kids. They saw their father every other weekend."

"What about his business associates? What do you know about them?"

"There were people who were around him recently," I said. "I didn't know them or about the businesses they were in. We were divorced, and I wasn't privy to his everyday life, only what he chose to tell me, which wasn't much."

"When you brought the kids to him, did you drop them off at the door?"

"I usually went inside with them, talked for a little bit, and then left," I said.

I was hoping that the detectives were getting the message that Darren and I didn't have a hateful relationship, and we didn't. I didn't care enough about him to hate him.

"Look," I said, cutting to the chase, "we had stuff going on during our marriage and after we separated, but that was in the past. We were getting along fine when he died."

"Stuff?"

I waited for them to bring up the stabbing from two years earlier, when Darren attacked me in our kitchen after my father died and I'd cut him with a paring knife. Surely they knew about it. The police report was on file downtown. When they didn't say anything, I brought it up.

"Darren and I had a history of domestic violence," I said. "There was a stabbing. It was a couple of years ago, just before we separated. He attacked me. I cut him. There were other fights. We abused each other verbally. But that was long over. That ended with the marriage. I had no reason to hurt Darren. I had no desire for my kids to be without a dad. I just recently lost my dad, and I know how painful it is."

The detectives had packed up Darren's computer and were taking it to the crime lab to have it examined, they said. "Did he have more than one?" I had no idea. Did I know where he kept his paper-work? Sorry, no.

"What did you know about his business dealings?"

"He had new people in his life," I said. "There was some deal he was working on with a bank in New York. That's what he said. He didn't give me any details."

The detectives asked if it was unusual for Darren to carry large amounts of cash with him. No, I said. He often carried rolls of hundred-dollar bills. That was one of the ways he tried to impress people. They said he had $4,000 in his pocket on the night he was shot. I don't know what the police were thinking, but I felt certain that Darren probably owed someone a lot of money. Maybe the cash he was carrying was to pay part of his debt. I'd seen him do that before, pay people a few thousand dollars to keep them off his back for a while. Was that the "business dinner" he told me about? For the first time since the shooting, it occurred to me that my kids could have been in the car with Darren when he was killed. Both had been with him at some point that day. What if the killer had been stalking him, following all of his movements, until he finally had a good shot in the garage? Sydney had been with Darren that same evening. What if she had been in the car when the hit man saw his opportunity? My little girl could have been killed as well. I shuddered at the thought and felt a sudden rage toward Darren. *What kind of people were you involved with?* I wondered. *How could you have been so careless to have relationships with people like that and put yourself and, much worse, your children at risk?*

The detectives asked about the last time Darren and I had spo-ken. He stopped at the pharmacy, I said. It was a busy night. I had lots of prescriptions to fill. I was behind the counter when Darren came in. We talked between customers. When he wasn't talking to me, he was walking around the pharmacy, talking on his cell phone. I asked the detectives if they'd checked his phone records. I guess it was a silly question. "We talked to all the people he was talking to that night," one said.

The detectives and I talked for an hour or so, until there didn't seem to be anything left to say. They offered to escort me to my car and led me out through the garage. Was that a coincidence? I don't think so. The garage was a mess, piled high with trash bags full of I don't know what. As I looked around I noticed blood spatter on the floor and realized I was standing on the spot where Darren was shot. The blood was his.

I couldn't get out of there fast enough.

30

Cold Case

*"What difference do it make if the thing you scared of
is real or not?"*

—*Toni Morrison*, Song of Solomon

AFTER THE CRIME scene tape came down, Darren's landlord called me to say he had a new renter and the condo had to be cleaned out. Would I be willing to do it? If not me, then who? "Yes," I said. "I'll do it." The sooner the better, the landlord said. For the next week, before and after work at the pharmacy, I went to the condo and packed things until I was too exhausted to move. I boxed up pots and pans and wrapped dishes and glasses in newspaper. I tossed out photographs and books and magazines and knickknacks. Clothes? Good Lord! Darren owned enough designer suits and shirts and ties to open an upscale men's clothing store. Half of his things were hung neatly on wooden hangers in his closet. The rest were strewn around his bedroom—on his bed, over his chair—just like when we were married. His stepfather took some of the clothing, and I donated the rest of his belongings to charity. What was I going to do? Save them for when my son grew up in ten years?

After days of cleaning out closets, I tackled Darren's dresser drawers. That man must have owned two hundred pairs of silk socks, all of them black. And underwear? He had every color and style imaginable. When the dresser drawers were empty and his clothes packed neatly in boxes, I opened the top drawer of his nightstand. "What is this?" I cried. The drawer was filled with condoms—every kind imaginable. Latex condoms. Textured condoms. Colored condoms. Charity condoms. Flavored condoms. Glow-in-the-dark condoms. Skyn condoms "for that Skyn-to-Skyn sensation." Tossed in among them were business cards and slips of paper with women's names and phone numbers jotted on them. I slammed the drawer shut. "OK, Yamma," I said, "Enough is enough." *I'm his ex-wife and I'm going to spend my day cleaning out his stash of condoms? I don't think so.* I decided to leave that task to someone else.

The detectives continued to contact me with random questions, and I called them to ask about the status of their investigation. The answer was always the same. "Nothing new." I wanted the case to be solved. I even went so far as to go on the local television news, pleading for anyone who knew anything to come forward. A killer was on the loose, and I was terrified for the lives of my children and myself. With good reason, it turned out.

A month after Darren's murder, I was walking the dog around our condominium complex after dark. A man came up behind me and put his gloved hand over my mouth. *I'm dead,* I thought. The man's gravelly voice sounded muffled and distorted. He must have had something over his mouth, but he didn't mince words. "Keep talking about Darren's death and someone else in your family will be hurt," he said. When I say I thought my pounding heart was going to leap out of my throat, I'm not exaggerating. I couldn't speak if I had wanted to. I nodded my head up and down. He finally let go of me and I heard his shoes hit the pavement as he ran off in the opposite direction. I waited a moment before I turned around, but when I did all I could see was a shadow with a black ski mask over his head. I couldn't help but wonder if this was the last person Darren saw before he was killed. I was literally shuddering as I ran back to my place. My knees gave out once I got inside and I locked the door behind me. For some odd reason, I didn't call 9-1-1. What were the police going to do? My assailant was long gone and I couldn't identify him. After a sleepless night, the next morning I called one of the investigators working on Darren's case and told him what had happened. He offered to file a police report, but I declined for fear that the masked man would return.

By then, the police had interviewed everyone who knew anything about my relationship with Darren. I finally told them, "Look, I've given you a tremendous amount of information and answered every question you've asked me. You know I had nothing to do with Darren's death. Now please start looking for who did." Apparently they were satisfied that I had no earthly reason, no motive, to have Darren killed, because they stopped coming around. I still periodically call to inquire about the investigation.

Five years later, the case is still unsolved.

And there are still moments when I turn to see who is walking behind me.

31

Blessed

"You must be the change you wish to see in the world."
—*Mahatma Gandhi*

IT'S ODD THE way grief works. It comes in waves, even long after a loss. Just the other day, I was in the shower, thinking about my story, and I was suddenly overcome with sadness. The feeling was as raw and as deep as when I first learned I'd lost my father. As the warm water washed over my body, I was taken back to that night in Dad's hospital room, as I lay there holding his breathless body. My thoughts then took me to the morning in the intensive care unit when I went to Darren's bed and realized he had died. The pain in my body was agonizing, and I sank to the floor, sobbing. How could I feel so much anguish, so many years later, over two men who mistreated me, two men who could be so insensitive and so very cruel? As I knelt there on the shower floor, with tears flooding my face, I found myself wondering if Dad would be proud of the woman I'd become. I found myself wondering if Darren would approve of the way I'm raising our children. The answer is that I just don't know.

After Darren died, I did some real soul-searching. I'd read enough and listened enough to finally understand that unless I made changes in my own behavior, my life's path would always lead to another abuser. It was in my James Brown genes. If I were ever going to find true love and real happiness, I had to first learn to love and respect myself. So I made a conscious decision to turn the volume down on the negative things Darren had said that were still stuck in my head. *You're ugly. You're stupid. You can't do anything right.* And every time I heard his voice, belittling or berating me, I'd turn my attention to something that validated me as a good and able person, perhaps a loving look or gesture from my children or a kind word from a colleague or friend.

Today, I try to live by the words of Stephen King in his book *On Writing*: "You can, you should, and if you're brave enough to start, *you will.*" Well, I think I'm finally brave enough to want the life I deserve.

I'm currently in a healthy, loving relationship with a God-fearing man I met at a Fourth of July picnic in 2011. Dejuan Alexander is a singer and songwriter. Our love of music drew us to one another, and now we're engaged. Dejuan is a totally different man than Darren. He is kind and gentle, and he encourages me to be myself. Most important, he loves my children. I pray that he is in our lives forever, but I'm taking it one step, one day at a time. People keep asking, "When's the wedding?" I say, "Who has time for a wedding? I'm a busy woman!" As much as I know I want to marry Dejuan, I'm still a little gun-shy. But it's getting better. I'll know when the time is right.

My children still struggle with Darren being gone. But children are resilient, and mine are doing well. Sydney is in high school. I can hardly believe she's talking about colleges and getting ready to drive. Carrington is an active kid and a great baseball player, just like his Dad said he was at that age. We certainly don't live the lifestyle we did with Darren. I work at a pharmacy and live by my father's lyrics: "Don't give me nothing. Open up the door, I will get it myself." But we have what's important. We have each other. And we have love.

My father's estate remains in limbo, tied up in litigation as of early 2014, but I work every day to make sure his legacy lives on. I long to see his Beech Island home turned into the museum he wanted, and Deanna and I have kept his holiday turkey and toy giveaways alive. I advocate for music in schools with the James Brown Family Foundation and am pushing ahead to make sure the underprivileged children from South Carolina and Georgia receive Dad's gift of an education. I met with Tate Taylor, the director of the film *The Help*; he and the producer Brian Grazer are making a movie about Dad, slated for a fall 2014 release, and they've asked Deanna and me to consult on the project. I'm thrilled at the prospect of being able to offer my perception of events and of who my father really was, and I'm grateful that we're being included in the project. Chadwick Boseman, who played Jackie Robinson in the biopic 42, plays Dad. I think he's the perfect choice.

I'm not sure what it will be like, watching my father's life play out again, this time on the big screen, but I'm pretty sure I'll handle it just fine. A few years ago, shortly after Darren's death, I met a man. I knew he wasn't someone who would be in my life forever, but he gave me the greatest gift. He taught me how to walk with God. That journey has taught me to go into my heart in search of myself and ultimately brought me to a place of strength.

I have forgiven both Darren and my dad. Realizing their vulnerabilities has been really enlightening. Yes, both of them hurt me deeply. They did bad things and they did a lot of damage, but they weren't bad people. They were wounded people. Neither of them had ever felt truly loved, so how could they possibly be capable of giving love? I finally understand that it wasn't me they didn't love. They didn't know how to love. And I can live with that. In many ways, that realization has set me free from the burdens of my past.

When I think about my life today, I think about where I came from and who I've become. A child who had had plenty of privilege and equal amounts of disappointment; a girl who was treated royally because of her heritage yet struggled with her own self-worth; a woman who had always longed for her father's love and approval and now, finally, loves and approves of herself.

I am Yamma Brown.

I say it loud. I say it proud.

INDEX